# Take My Hands!

by

Diana Schrader

Publishing House
St. Louis

*To Donna—
whose love and friendship gave me the gift of time—
this book is most gratefully and lovingly dedicated!*

Copyright © 1980 CPH
Concordia Publishing House

Manufactured in the United States of America

All rights reserved

No portion of this book may be reproduced in any form, except for brief quotations, without the written permission of the publisher.

# Table of Contents

**Introduction** — 5

**The Church Year**
- Advent — 9
- Christmas — 11
- Epiphany — 16
- Lent — 19
- Palm Sunday — 20
- Maundy Thursday — 21
- Peter's denial — 22
- Good Friday — 23
- Easter — 25
- Ascension — 27
- Pentecost — 30

**Other Holidays**
- Thanksgiving — 33
- Mother's Day — 34
- Father's Day — 36

**The Old Testament**
- Creation — 39
- Noah — 41
- Joseph — 44
- Moses — 47
- David — 51
- Solomon — 54
- Fiery Furnace — 55
- Daniel — 58
- Jonah — 59

**The New Testament**
- Christ's Ministry — 61
- The Temptation of Christ — 62
- Marriage at Cana — 62
- Lord's Prayer — 63
- Love — 64
- Disciples and Apostles — 68
- Parables — 70

Appendix I — 79
Appendix II — 80

## Introduction

God gave His children special gifts—the ability to imagine, the process of thought to utilize that imagination, and uniquely formed hands to create what the mind's eye sees.

Through art projects, children can witness for Christ. They can give their feelings, their beliefs, and their knowledge physical form. It is free expression—no right or wrong solutions!

The art projects presented in this book have been written to help you add something special to your Bible study program. Most of the projects are adaptable to all grades. Some are geared to specific age groups. All have been written to provide your students with a variety of ways to praise and glorify their God with their imaginations and their hands.

*To God be the glory forever!*

*Take my hands and let them move
At the impulse of Thy love . . .*

# Chapter 1: The Church Year

## ADVENT

*Hark the glad sound!*
*    The Savior comes,*
*The Savior promised long;*
*Let every heart prepare a throne*
*    And every voice a song.*

*Philip Doddridge*

### 1. The Advent Calendar *(4—8) Variation for K—3*

The Advent Calendar is one way in which children—and adults—can prepare for the coming of Christmas. Calendars can be purchased commercially but, unfortunately, most of these depict the secular aspects of the holiday rather than verses or symbols representative of the true meaning of Christmas.

Younger children will find it especially enjoyable to use a calendar which they have made themselves.

**Materials Needed:** heavy construction paper, scissors, glue, old Christmas cards (not secular themes), craft knife, rulers, newspapers, and rickrack (optional).

**How to Do It:**
a. Instruct the children to draw a house on a large sheet of construction paper and cut it out with a scissors.
b. With a ruler, children should draw 23 windows any place they wish. There will be one window for every day from December 1 to December 23. The windows may vary in size and shape or may all be uniform.
c. A large door should be drawn for December 24.
d. A line should be drawn down the center of each window.
e. Place the house on a stack of newspapers and, using a craft knife or single-edge razor blade, students should carefully slit across the top, bottom, and center of each window. CAUTION STUDENTS *NOT* TO CUT THE SIDES!
f. The top, bottom, and ONE SIDE of the door should also be cut.
g. The house, windows, and door may be trimmed with ribbon or other rickrack.
h. Instruct the children to lay the house on another sheet of construction paper, trace the outline, and cut it out. This is then glued to the BACK of the original house.
i. Each window and door is CAREFULLY opened so the other piece of construction paper is visible.
j. Various pictures should be cut from the Christmas cards and glued inside each window. A picture of the Christ Child is glued inside the doorway.
k. Windows and door are reclosed. Tape if they pop open.

*Teacher Note:* Encourage students to use their calendars as part of daily family devotions.

**Variation:** *K—3* **Advent Stable Scene Calendar**

If the motor skills of younger students have not developed sufficiently to attempt the Advent Calendar House, this activity is an excellent alternative.

**Materials Needed:** tagboard or heavy construction paper, old Christmas cards, scissors, and envelopes.

Children cut out 23 figures (Mary, Joseph, Christ Child, shepherds, angels, etc.) from old Christmas cards. Each piece should be numbered on the back (1—23), the Christ Child numbered 24. Pieces should be placed in an envelope.

Allow children to draw or paint a stable scene on a sheet of tagboard or construction paper. Attach the envelope of figures to the back of the scene.

Each day in Advent a piece is added to the scene until, on December 24, the Christ Child is placed on the picture.

Cut from Christmas Card    Back of Christmas card cutout

**Figure 1**

**Variation II:** *grade 6—8* Instead of using pictures in the house windows, give each student a ditto with squares containing Bible verses. These are cut out and glued into each window. A Bible verse is read each day a window is opened.

## 2. Advent Wreaths and Devotionals K—8

The use of the Advent wreath is probably one of the most common of family customs. The custom—probably of German origin—has become a tradition in thousands of Christian homes and churches.

The wreath—made with various types of evergreen—symbolizes the eternity of God and of the human soul. The most common form of wreath consists of four candles—one for each Sunday in Advent.

The Advent wreath was once the center of family devotions—a custom which, unfortunately, has been crowded out by Santas and cute little elves. This project will give families the encouragement to follow this custom once more.

**Materials Needed:** self-hardening clay, Bake-O-Clay or Baker's Clay, candles (may be supplied by children), paint.

**How to Do It:**
a. Using the clay provided, children make a "wreath" by rolling the clay into a snake shape and attaching both ends to form a circle. Candles should be pressed into the soft clay and then removed—forming the holders for the candles.
b. Clay should be allowed to dry—or bake according to instructions.
c. When clay is hard—and cool—children can paint their wreaths.
d. When paint is dry, candles are placed in holders.

**Variation:** Children might enjoy adding clay "leaves" and "berries" by shaping the clay and pressing them into the circle form before drying.

**Devotionals:**

*K—3:* Duplicate several Bible passages and prayers as shown in Fig. 2.

---

[Page 3]

Silent Night, Holy night!
All is calm, all is bright,
Round yon Virgin Mother and Child.
Holy infant, so tender and mild,
Sleep in heavenly peace, Sleep in heavenly peace.

[Page 2]

Christmas is Jesus' Birthday!

Dear Jesus, Help me to remember that we celebrate Christmas because You were born. Help me to remember that You are Christmas. Amen.

FOLD 2

FOLD 1

[Page 4]

Dear Jesus, Everyday we see Santas and pink Christmas trees, toys and Christmas wrappings. Help us to remember that these things are not important. Help us to remember that Christmas would still come even if we didn't have all these things. Amen.

[Page 1]

MY ADVENT DEVOTIONS

**Figure 2**

Children can draw a picture for the cover and staple or tie the booklet pages together.

*4—8:* Older students should be encouraged to copy favorite passages and write several original prayers to be used at family devotions when Advent candles are lit.

*Verily I say unto you, Inasmuch as ye have done it unto one of the least of these My brethren, ye have done it unto Me.*

Matthew 25:40 KJV

## 3. Christmas Surprise Boxes K—8

Sharing is a wonderful attribute—especially at Christmas time. This project will enable children to create something which will help make another person's Christmas a bit brighter.

**Materials Needed:** gift boxes, ribbons, brightly colored wrapping paper, drawing paper, paints or other coloring medium, scissors, material scraps.

**How to Do It:**
a. Cut a hole in the side of the box large enough to allow a fist to go in and out. (See Fig. 3.)

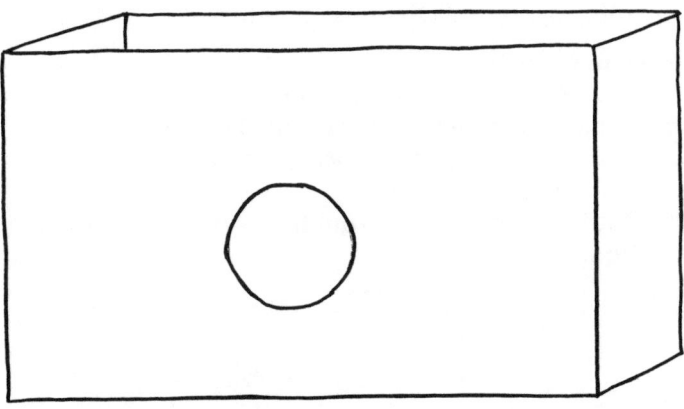

Hole is covered from the INSIDE with a piece of scrap material.

**Figure 3**

b. Students should cut a piece of material which will be large enough to serve as a "curtain" for the window. The material should be taped to the INSIDE of the box to cover the hole.
c. Instruct students to create various puzzles, pictures, mazes, dot-to-dot pictures, Bible story booklets, etc., which are all based on the Bible. Each piece is rolled up, tied with a ribbon, and placed into the box.*

d. Children then tape or glue wrapping to the box and decorate with a ribbon or other decoration.

*If finances permit, the class may like to purchase small commercial toys or games to include in the boxes.

Completed boxes are then distributed to a children's home or hospital (obtain permission first).

## CHRISTMAS

*For unto you is born this day in the city of David a Savior, which is Christ the Lord.*

Luke 2:11 KJV

## 4. Sand Casting K—8

**Materials Needed:** plaster of paris, water, fine sand, newspaper, and chicken wire (optional).

From home: aluminum baking pans and crèche figures—the inexpensive plastic type.

**How to Do It:**
a. Cover the work area with newspaper.
b. Each student should fill an aluminum baking pan halfway with damp sand. Be sure sand is moistened throughout.
c. Smooth the sand with a straight edge.
d. The crèche figures are embedded into the damp sand, making a clean, clear impression. If children are dissatisfied with the arrangement, the sand can be smoothed and another arrangement tried.
e. When the children are satisfied with their arrangements, objects are put aside.
f. Plaster of paris is mixed with water until it is the consistency of pancake batter. (Younger students can do this just as well as older students, so don't be afraid to let them try.)
g. When plaster is ready, it is very carefully poured into each impression made. Children should do this SLOWLY to be sure that all cracks and crevices are filled with plaster.
h. When impressions are filled, children should continue to pour the plaster until there is approximately ½ inch of plaster in the pan.
i. At this point a piece of chicken wire may be added for extra support.
j. Children continue to pour plaster until an inch or more has been accumulated in the pan. A bent wire is embedded into the soft plaster for a hanger.
k. The plaster should be allowed to dry for several hours before continuing. After plaster has dried, the frame is cut or bent away, and the plaster piece is

removed from the sand.
l. Children should brush excess sand from the casting.
m. The plaster piece may be sprayed with a fixative and displayed as is or children may wish to paint them.

## 5. Bible Ornaments K—8

Through the years, families have turned away from the Christmas tradition of making ornaments for the tree. Ornaments have become more and more representative of the secular aspects of the season and, because many of them are expensive, some children are even forbidden to help trim the tree for fear of little hands dropping the fragile pieces.

**Materials Needed:** scrap paper, heavy cardboard, fine sandpaper, craft knives or single-edge razor blades, acrylic paints, felt scraps, sequins and other rickrack, hole punchers, old Christmas cards, yarn and glue.

**How to Do It:**
a. Let children experiment with scrap paper to form various symmetrical designs. (See Fig. 4.)

b. Once the children have developed designs with which they are satisfied, designs may be traced onto cardboard and cut out using single-edge razor blades or craft knives.
c. Fine sandpaper is used to smooth out any rough edges.
d. A hole is punched at the top of each ornament.
e. Ornaments should be painted on both sides—allowing one side to dry before painting the other.
f. Pictures depicting the birth of Christ or other Biblical stories are glued onto the ornaments.
g. Ornaments are then trimmed with yarn, ribbon, sequins or other rickrack.
h. A loop of yarn is tied to the ornament for hanging.

**Variation:** K—3
Substitute heavy construction paper for cardboard so children can use scissors instead of razor blades OR give children several pre-cut cardboard pieces which they can decorate.

*But Mary kept all these things, and pondered them in her heart.*
*Luke 2:19 KJV*

## 6. Madonna and Child K—8

**Materials Needed:** large paper plates, glue, tinsel, yarn, or ribbon.

**How to Do It:**
a. Cut a 6-inch circle for Mary's head.
b. Cut a 5-inch circle for the Christ Child's head.
c. Cut a 4-inch section for Mary's "collar" and a 3-inch section for the child's.
d. Cut the arm of Mary from half a plate as shown in Figure 5a.

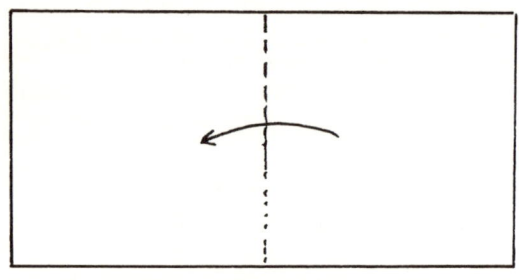
A. Fold paper in half

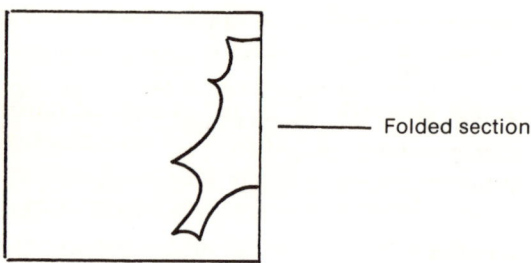
B. Draw half design along folded section and cut out.

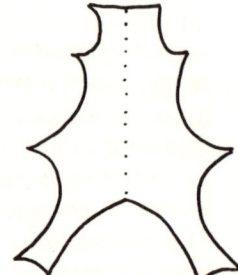
C. Unfold completed design and paint.

**Figure 4**

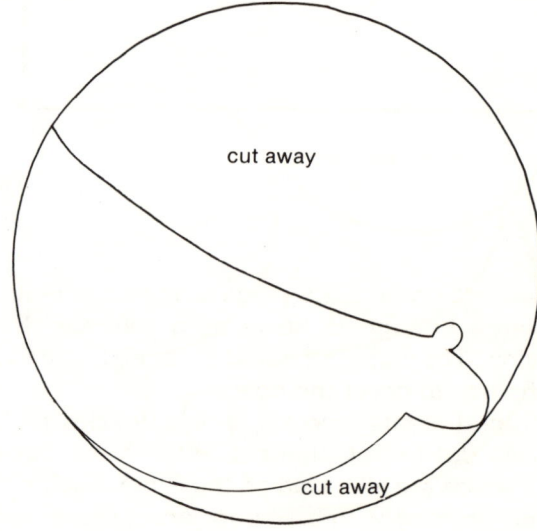
**Figure 5A**

e. Cut a quarter-moon shape for the base of Mary's hair (see Fig. 5b).

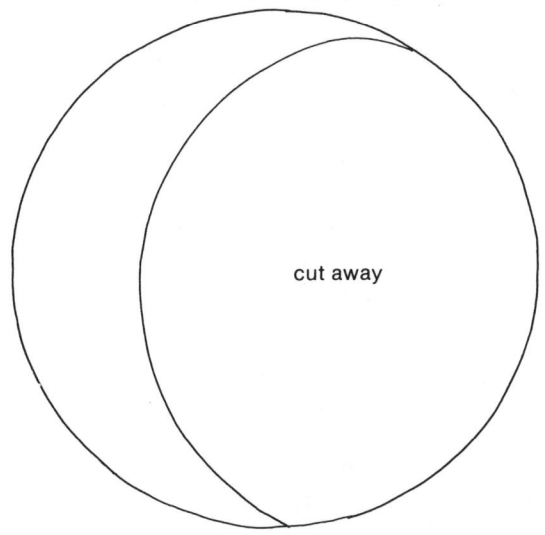

**Figure 5B**

f. The halo for the Christ Child is made from a plate rim trimmed with silver or gold tinsel.
g. Hair can be made from yarn or ribbon which is cut and curled with a scissor.
h. Features of each face are made from construction paper.
i. Glue finished piece onto an 18" x 25" sheet of painted cardboard or heavy construction paper.

**Variation:** Younger children can easily attempt this project but may need pieces pre-cut first.

MADONNA AND CHILD

**Figure 5C**

*O sing unto the Lord a new song; for He hath done marvelous things.*
*Psalm 98:1 KJV*

### 7. Christmas Carol Booklet K—8

**Materials Needed:** 9" x 12" sheets of construction paper, 10" x 13" pieces of tagboard, crayons or paints, scissors and glue.

**How to Do It:**
a. Using paints or other coloring medium, children should make the cover of the book as illustrative of the Christmas season as possible.
b. Christmas hymns and carols (words and melodies), which have been copied and run off by the teacher, are glued to colorful pieces of construction paper and included in the booklets.
c. Holes are punched into tagboard covers and pages and tied together with yarn.

**Variation:** 6—8
Older students might be given melodies only and encouraged to write their own lyrics—or vice versa. Booklets made by older children might also be included as part of the Gift Booklets. (See Activity 8.)

*It is more blessed to give than to receive.*
*Acts 20:35 KJV*

### 8. Gift Booklets K—8 (To be distributed in homes for the aged)

**Materials Needed:** 12" x 18" sheets of cardboard or tagboard, 12" x 18" sheets of construction paper, acrylic paints, old Christmas cards, winter scenes, pictures of flowers, etc., yarn or heavy cord.

**How to Do It:**
a. Cover
(1) Paint two pieces of cardboard with several coats of acrylic paint—allowing one coat to dry before applying another.
(2) After paint has dried *completely,* students may add appropriate designs. (See below.)*
  Bells—Cut a styrofoam cup in half.
    —Glue ribbon or fringe around bottom and top edges of both halves. Add bows to top. Glue to covers.
  Crèche Scene—Cut out felt pieces according to pattern shown in Fig. 6.

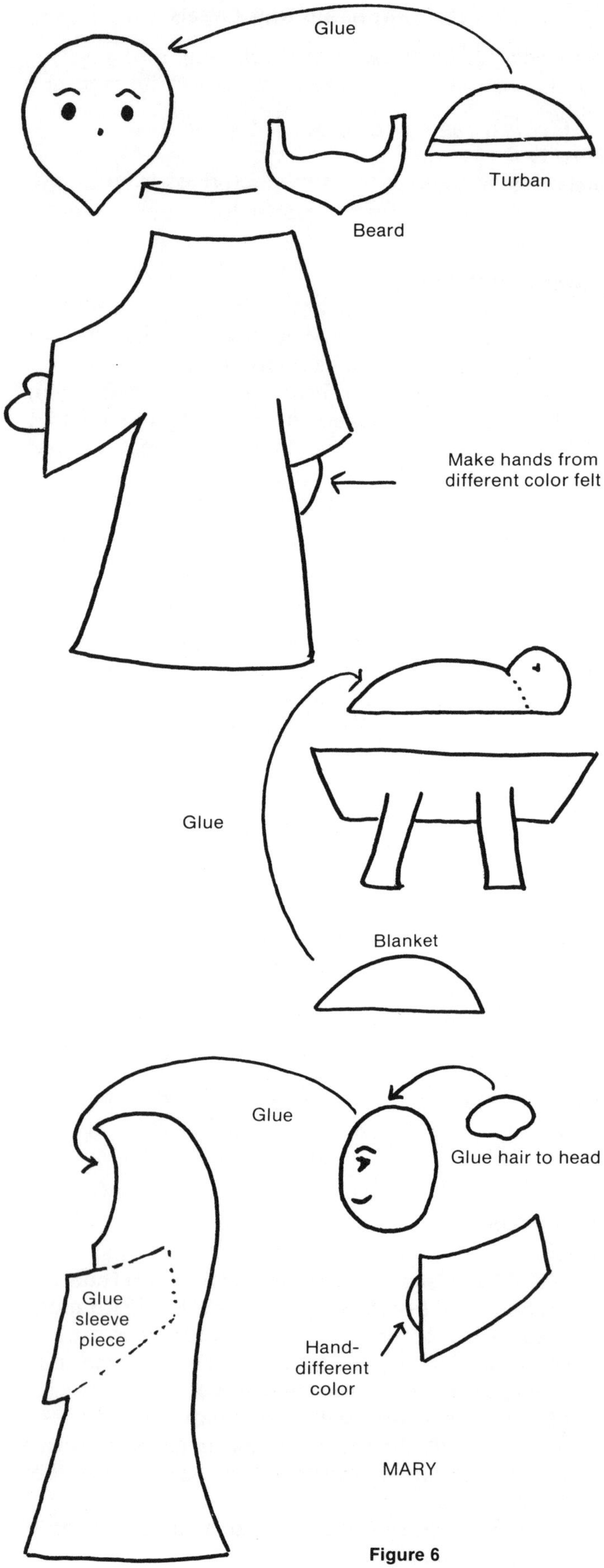

Word Motif—Use pieces of cardboard and cut out words associated with the Christmas season (JOY, PEACE, LOVE, GOOD NEWS, etc.). Paint and decorate with rickrack.

*These are merely suggestions. Children should be encouraged to use their imaginations.

b. Inside
(1) Pictures from cards or magazines are glued to pieces of construction paper.
(2) Bible verses, hymns, prayers, or inspirational poems should be copied and glued to each picture. (The adult leader may copy verses and duplicate for younger students.)

c. Binding
(1) Covers should be creased approximately 1 inch from the edges.
(2) Using hole puncher, students should make holes approximately one inch apart in *both* covers and all pages.
(3) A basic binding stitch (Fig. 7) is used to bind all materials together.

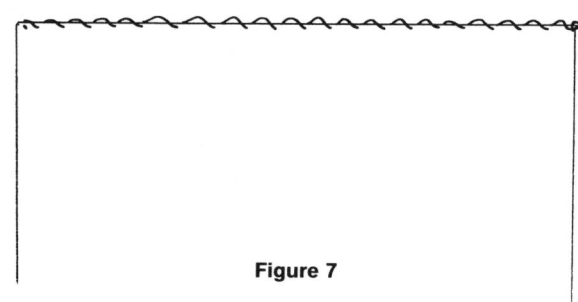

Figure 7

## 9. Christmas Hangings K—8

**Materials Needed:** paper, white string, glue, starch, and acrylic paints.

**How to Do It:**
a. Have students draw a Christmas design on paper.
b. Dip pieces of white string into a mixture of glue and starch (half and half to a consistency of heavy cream).
c. CAREFULLY place wet string along the lines of the drawn design.
d. When the design is completely dry, students may paint the string with acrylics.
e. Design is cut out completely and a loop of yarn glued to the top for hanging.

**Variation:** Draw a design on wax paper or aluminum foil with felt-tipped pens and follow directions 2 and 3.

When the design is completely dry, it can be lifted off the foil or wax paper. Tissue paper is then glued to the back of the design to create a "stained glass" effect.

Figure 6

*And suddenly there was with the angel a multitude of the heavenly host.*

*Luke 2:13 KJV*

## 10. Angels

### 10¹ Foil Angel

**Materials Needed:** cardboard, aluminum foil, 2" foam balls, yarn, pipe cleaners, black construction paper and white glue.

**How to Do It:**

a. Cut a 12" pie wedge from a piece of cardboard. The curved end of the pie piece should be 8½" across. (See Fig. 8.)

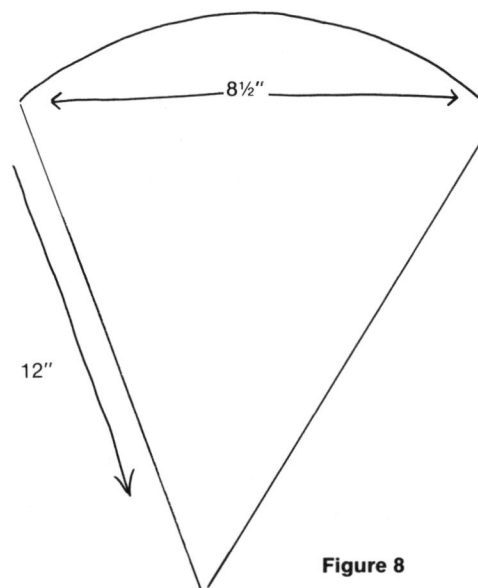

**Figure 8**

b. Form a cone from the "pie wedge" so it has a 2½" base. Secure with glue.
c. Cut 3 inches off the top of the cone. Cover the remaining section with aluminum foil.
d. A 12-inch pipe cleaner serves as the angel's arms. Have students loop the ends of the pipe cleaner to simulate hands. Cover the arms—NOT THE HANDS—with with aluminum foil for "sleeves."
e. A circle—9 inches in diameter—is cut from aluminum foil and then cut in half.
f. Each half circle is fringed by cutting edges 3 inches toward the center.
g. Each semi-circle is folded in a fan shape and attached to the body cone with glue and secured with tape until glue dries.
h. A 2-inch styrofoam ball serves as the angel's head.
i. Glue on yarn for hair and construction paper for facial features. Attach the head to the cone with glue.
j. A songbook can be constructed from construction paper and glued to the angel's hands.

### 10² Cardboard Roll Angels

**Materials Needed:** cardboard rolls—all sizes, acrylic paints, cotton, glitter, braid, or other rickrack and white glue.

**How to Do It:**

a. Have children cut twelve ½-inch rings from a cardboard tube as shown in Figure 9.

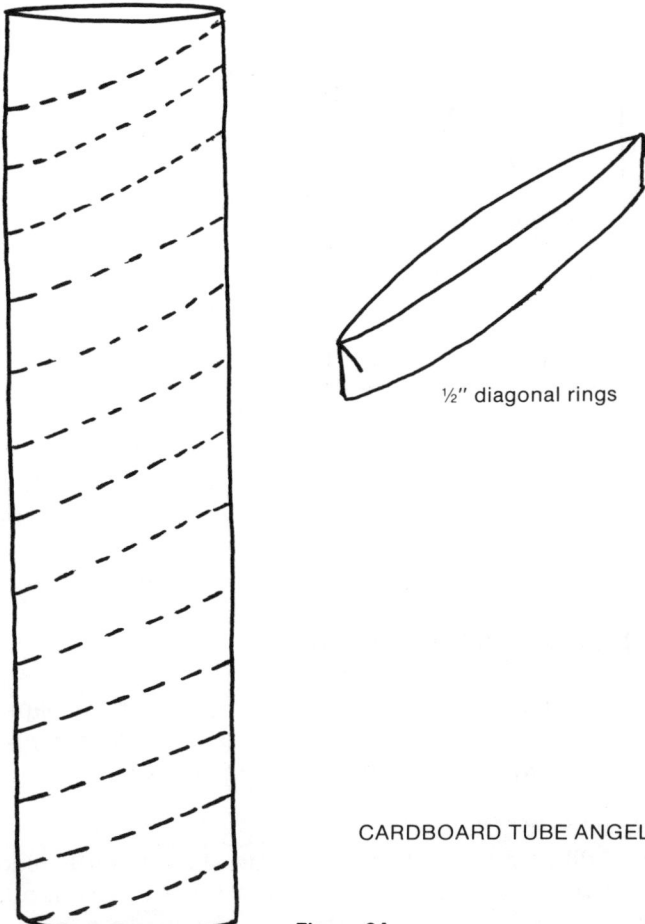

½" diagonal rings

CARDBOARD TUBE ANGEL

**Figure 9A**

b. The pointed ends of six rings are glued to the bottom of the body which is formed from a 4½-inch long tube. The other six rings are glued above and between the first six.
c. Students should cut two more rings for the wings and glue these in place at the back of the body.
d. Arms can be made from a strip of cardboard glued to the back and sides of the body and bent to desired position.
e. The angel's head is made from a cylinder approximately 1¼ inches in length and covered front and back by cardboard circles. The front circle is painted and facial features added. The head is glued to the body.
f. Paint and decorate the angel as desired. Cotton is added to the head for hair.

**TUBE ANGEL**

**Figure 9B**

## EPIPHANY

*Behold, there came Wise Men from the East to Jerusalem, Saying where is He that is born King of the Jews? for we have seen His star in the East, and are come to worship Him.*

Matthew 2:1-2 KJV

### 11. Wise Man Plaque  4—8

**Materials Needed:** heavy cardboard, fabric, or paper towels toothpicks, pins, cotton, acrylic paints and brushes, white craft glue, cord and scissors.

### How to Do It:

a. Following the pattern in Figure 10, students make two body parts from heavy cardboard and cut out.

b. For the head, students should cut out two oval pieces of cardboard—each approximately 2½ inches long. A nose should be provided for. (Make sure body pieces and heads are facing the same way.)

c. Glue several pieces of cotton onto one body piece and one head piece. Then glue the other halves onto the cotton to form a "sandwich." This will give the figure a 3D effect.

d. Place the white craft glue (or draping solution) into a pan for easy handling.

e. Dip a small piece of paper toweling or fabric into the glue solution and cover the head. Press the paper towel tight against the cardboard. Overlap the excess towel to the back and pin to hold until dry. Glue head to body—tape to secure.

f. Two arms (see Fig. 11) should be cut from cardboard.

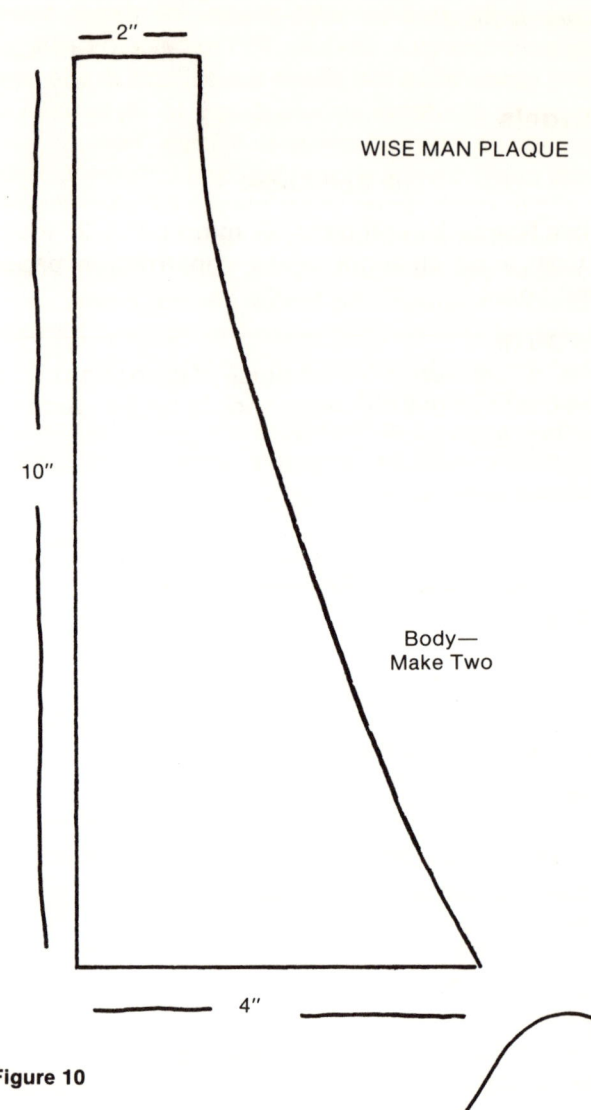

WISE MAN PLAQUE

Body— Make Two

**Figure 10**

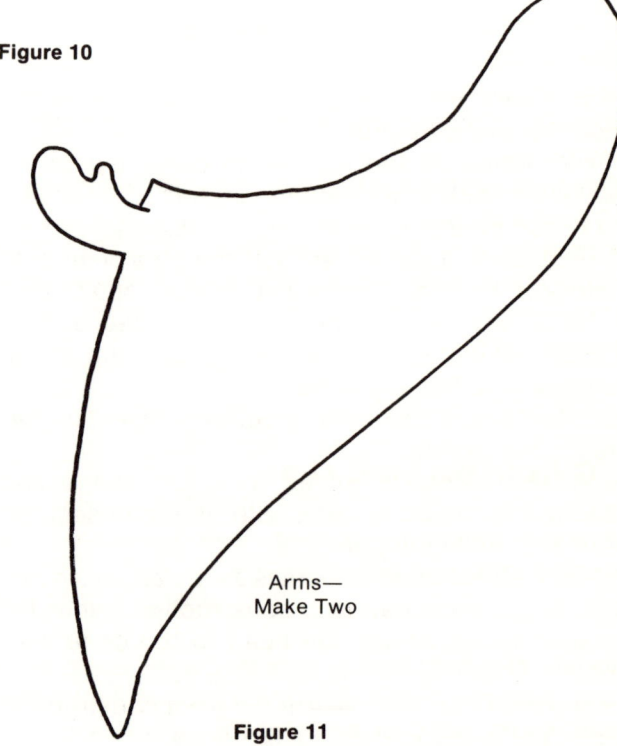

Arms— Make Two

**Figure 11**

16

g. Follow number 5 to cover the *hands*.
h. Cover both sleeves with pieces of paper towel dipped in the glue mixture. Pin excess to back.
i. Form robes from the paper towels and drape over the body. Students should drape to form folds in the robe and turned under to form a "hem."
j. Extra paper towels should be used to form a cloak.
k. Beard is made from short pieces of cord dipped into solution and attached to face.
l. A turban can be made from a strip of paper towel, dipped in solution and folded several times.
m. The arms are attached when the figure is partially dry—one arm to the back of the figure, the other is attached to the front.
n. Students can paint the figure when it is completely dry and mount on a heavy sheet of cardboard covered with fabric.

## 12. Star K—8

**Materials Needed:** metallic foil or gold or silver wrapping paper, picture-hanging wire, stapler, scissors, Christmas balls, or other decoration.

**How to Do It:**
a. Students first cut out two circles from the foil—one circle 6 inches in diameter, the other 5½ inches. This should be done *before* project time for younger students.
b. Each circle is divided into six equal pie wedges and each segment cut within one inch of the center of the circle.
c. A ½-inch hole is cut out of the center of each circle.
d. The points of the star are formed by bending back each segment in pinwheel fashion and stapling the corners. (Caution the students not to crease the segments.)
e. The smaller star is placed on top of the larger so all 12 points show.
f. Attach a piece of wire to a Christmas ball or other decoration, and thread the wire through both stars—twisting it at the back of the larger star to secure the piece.

## 13. Gifts to the Lord 4—8

*And when they had opened their treasures, they presented unto Him gifts . . .*
                                        Matthew 2:11 KJV

**Materials Needed:** heavy construction paper, compasses, pictures from cards or magazines, white craft glue, scissors, needles, and thread.

**How to Do It:**
a. Instruct the students to draw 20 circles—all the same size—on heavy construction paper. (For best results, diameters should be no less than 5 inches.)
b. The centers of the circles should be marked.
c. Circles are cut out and folded toward the center on three "sides"—forming a triangle in the center of each (Fig. 12).

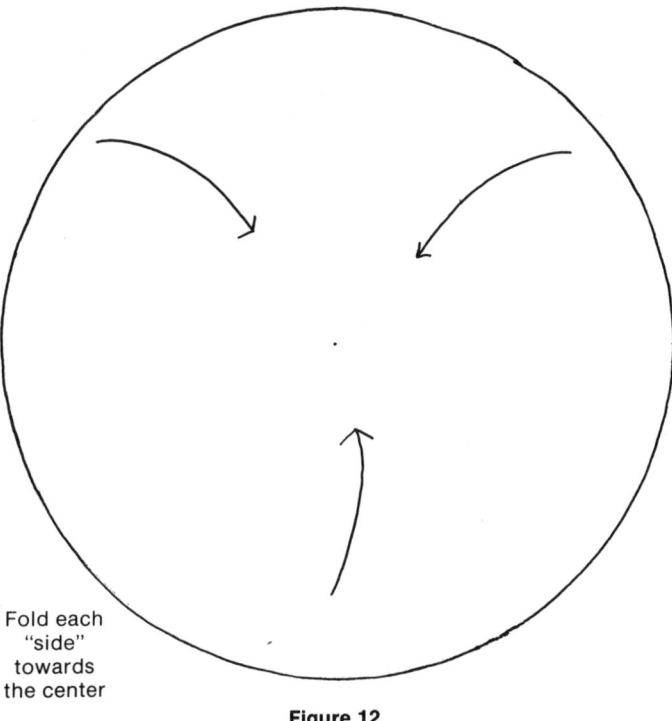

Fold each "side" towards the center

**Figure 12**

d. A picture showing something we can give to the Lord is glued in each triangle (Using various skills, showing kindness, money for offerings, caring for animals, etc.)
e. Ten of the circles are glued together by joining the sides as shown in Figure 13.

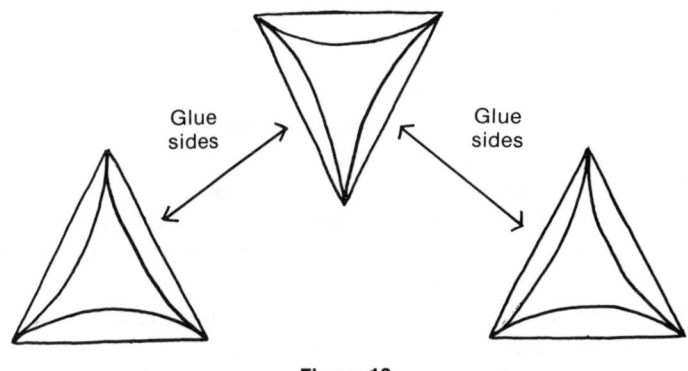

**Figure 13**

f. The sides of the first and 10th circles are glued together—forming an open circle of pieces. Allow to dry.
g. The remaining 10 pieces will form the two domes—consisting of five pieces each. Have children line up the remaining pieces in two rows of five—all triangles facing upward this time (Fig. 14).

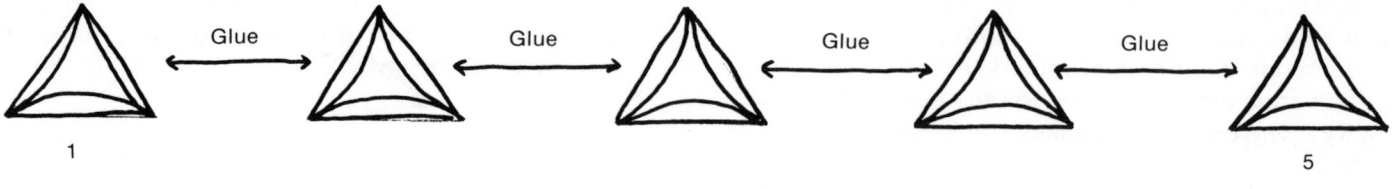

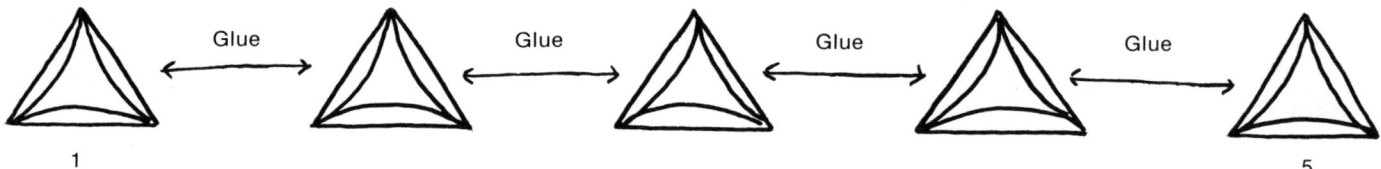

Glue sides of pieces 1 and 5 together.
This will create a dome.

**Figure 14**

h. The sides of the five pieces in each group are glued together as in step 5. This will result in two dome shapes.
i. The domes are glued to the top and bottom of the circular piece constructed in steps 5 and 6. Allow one dome to dry completely before attaching the second.
j. To hang, use heavy thread and push through one of the dome tops to form a secure loop.

**Variation:** K—3
a. Duplicate the pattern in Fig. 15.
b. Children cut out the pattern—being careful not to cut off the tabs.
c. BEFORE folding, a piece of yarn or thread should be pulled through the center of the top for hanging.
d. Pieces are folded to form a box shape, and tabs are secured with masking tape.
e. Pictures which illustrate gifts to Jesus are glued to each side of the box except the top.
f. When boxes are dry, they are ready for hanging.

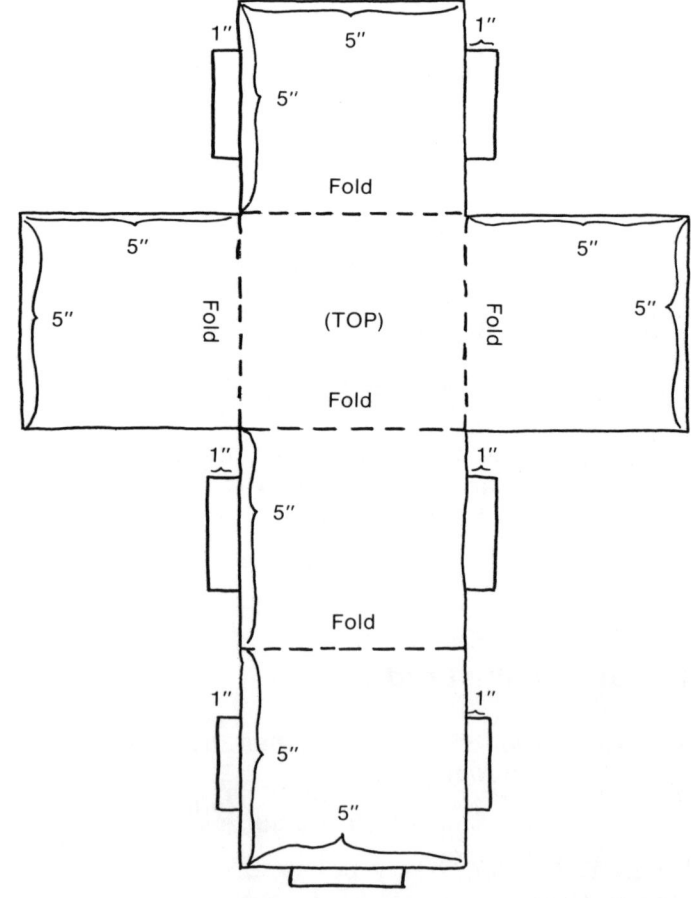

**Figure 15**

## LENT

The Lenten season, which begins on Ash Wednesday and continues until Easter, is a time of preparation for all Christians. During this time, all Christians are reminded of the reasons for Christ's coming, His death on the cross, and His final victory on Easter Sunday.

### 14. Lenten Calendar *4—8*

Here is a variation on the traditional Advent Calendar.

**Materials Needed:** tagboard, brown wrapping paper, acrylic paints, brushes, scissors, and glue.

**How to Do It:**
a. Wrapping paper should be cut to the size of the tagboard—allowing an inch more on all sides for an overlapping border.
b. Using acrylic paints, children draw an outline map of Jerusalem and surrounding areas in which Christ preached just before His death and resurrection.
c. After the map is completed and dry, children should cut out 40 windows (count the number of days between Ash Wednesday and Easter Sunday). Windows should be cut on *three sides only.*
d. Wrapping paper is glued to the back of tagboard background. Caution should be taken to avoid gluing window flaps to the tagboard.
e. Flaps are lifted and Bible verses or pictures illustrating Christ's ministry are drawn or glued in place.*
f. Flaps are closed and numbered for each day in Lent.
*The verses could include portions from the Sermon on the Mount, words from the cross, etc. Or suggest Bible references to be written in the windows. When these are opened, the student looks up the verse for that day.

### 15. Bread Dough Plaques *K—8*

*I am the vine, ye are the branches.*
John 15:5 KJV

**Materials Needed:** scrap wood, bread dough mixture (see Appendix), glue, acrylic paints, tacks and picture wire, fine sandpaper.

**How to Do It:**
a. Wood should be sanded to eliminate splinters.
b. Children may paint the wood or it may be left in its natural state. Attach wire hanger on the back with tacks.
c. Using the bread dough mixture, children form a vine with branches.
d. After this hardens, it is painted and glued to the piece of wood.
e. The Bible verse (John 15:5) is written in on the bottom. (You may wish to duplicate the verse for younger children if their writing skills have not developed sufficiently.)

### 16. Gift Baskets *K—8 (To be distributed to the elderly)*

*This is My commandment, That ye love one another, as I have loved you.*
John 15:12 KJV

**Materials Needed:** gallon bleach bottles, acrylic paints, glue, scissors, tagboard, material scraps, heavy yarn, tissue paper and Easter "grass," winged paper fasteners.

**How to Do It:**
a. Tops of the bleach bottles are cut off just below the handle. (This should be done before project time for younger children.)
b. Two holes are punched on opposite sides of the bottle rim (Fig. 16A).

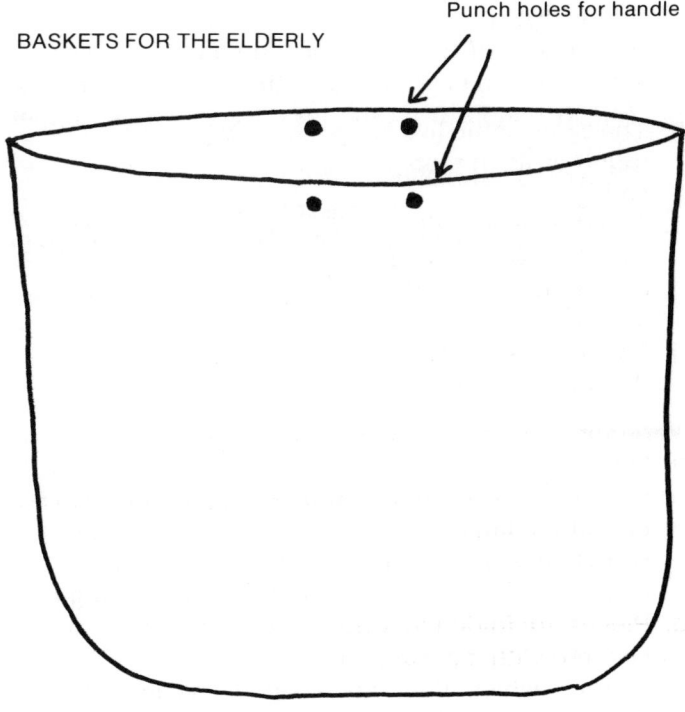

BASKETS FOR THE ELDERLY

GALLON BLEACH BOTTLE

Figure 16A

c. Children should paint and decorate with acrylics.
d. A circle—9 inches in diameter—is cut from tagboard and covered with material or painted.
e. Circle is cut to form connecting "petals" (petals should be no more than 2 inches deep) Fig. 16B

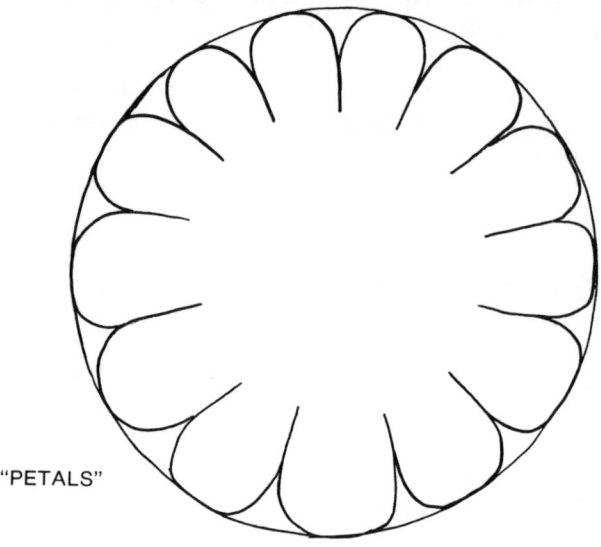

"PETALS"

**Figure 16B**

f. Glue bottle to center of circle. Allow to dry COMPLETELY.
g. Using colored tissued paper, students should form enough flowers to fit around the edge of the bottle. (Allow children to use their imaginations for flower patterns. Let them experiment with scrap paper first.)
h. Finished flowers are glued around the bottom edge of the bottle.
i. Cut a strip of tagboard for the handle. Punch two holes in both sides to match the holes in the bottle. Attach handle from the inside with winged paper fasteners.
j. Cover the handle with heavy yarn or ribbon.
k. Children can fill the baskets with booklets illustrating the Easter story, pictures with appropriate Bible verses, some fruit, etc.

## PALM SUNDAY

*And a very great multitude spread their garments in the way; others cut down branches from the trees and strewed them in the way.*

*Matthew 2:8 KJV*

### 17. Palm Trees K—8

**Materials Needed:** newspaper, wheat paste, acrylic paints, straight pins, cardboard, masking tape.

**How to Do It:**
a. Instruct students to roll up a sheet of newspaper and tape (the larger the roll, the bigger the finished tree).
b. The roll is wrapped in several layers on newspaper strips dipped in wheat paste.
c. While this is drying, students should make five or six palm leaves from cardboard.
d. The leaves are covered with strips dipped in wheat paste.
e. Leaves are pinned to the trunk and secured with strips of dipped newspaper.
f. Piece should be allowed to dry overnight.
g. When trees are dry, they can be painted. Bible verses are added to leaves with a felt-tipped pen.
h. A base can be made from self-hardening clay or rolls of paper dipped in the wheat-paste solution.

**Variation** K—3

**Materials Needed:** cardboard tubes, construction paper, newspaper, wheat paste, pins, and paint.

**How to Do It:**
a. Children wrap several layers of newspaper strips dipped in wheat paste around tube. They should also form a base so the tree will stand without support.
b. While this is drying, children can make several palm leaves from construction paper. Or you might give each child five duplicated leaves which they can color and cut out. (See Fig. 17.)

PALM TREES

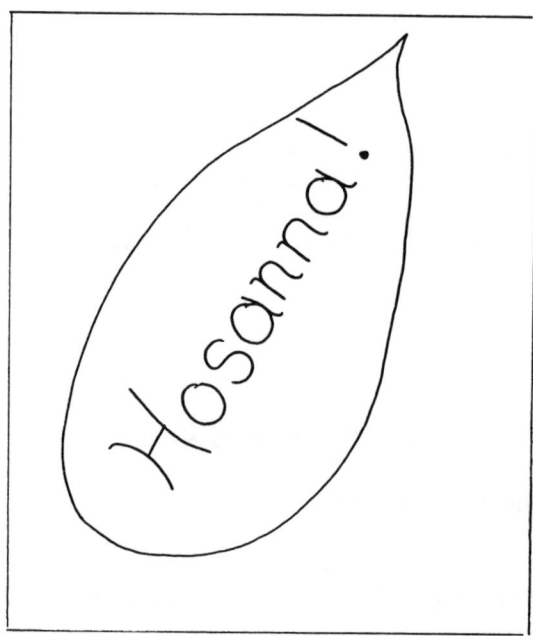

Palm Leaf—Children color and cut out.

**Figure 17**

c. Each leaf is pinned to the finished tree trunk.

## MAUNDY THURSDAY

*And they paid him 30 pieces of silver.*
Matthew 26:15 RSV

### 18. Betrayal Collage K—8

**Materials Needed:** construction paper, brown wrapping paper, newspapers, magazines, scissors and glue.

**How to Do It:**
a. Children should cut out the shape of a bag from the brown wrapping paper (Fig. 18).

BETRAYAL COLLAGE

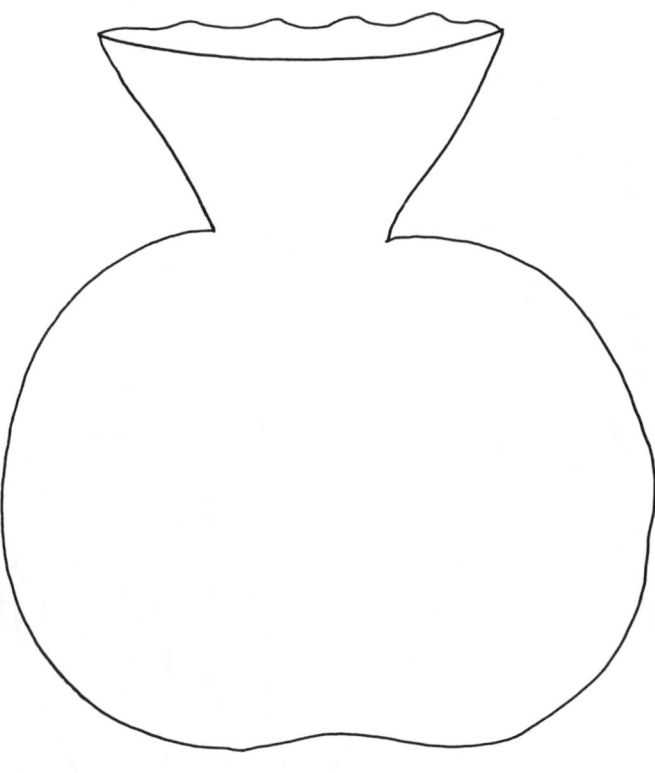

Figure 18

b. The bag is glued to a sheet of construction paper.
c. Thirty circles—all the same size—are cut from construction paper.
d. From newspapers and magazines, students cut out pictures which illustrate how people today betray Christ. Pictures are glued to the construction paper circles.
e. Circles are glued into the "bag"—overlapping if necessary.
f. Matthew 26:15 can be copied at the top or bottom of the finished picture.

### Variation K—3

Make a large "bag" shape and staple to a bulletin board. Give each child one or more circles (depending on the number of children in the class). Each child covers the circle with a picture which illustrates a way Christ is betrayed. Circles are attached to the bulletin board in the "bag."

When it is time to take the bulletin board down, give the circles back to the children and help them write a prayer on the back.

### 19. The Lord's Supper Banner 4—8

*Take, eat; this is My body . . . Drink ye all of it, for this is My blood of the new testament, which is shed for many for the remission of sins.*
Matthew 26:26-28 KJV

**Materials Needed:** material scraps, dowel rods, scissors, and glue.

**How to Do It:**
a. Let students experiment with various designs which would represent the Lord's Supper. (See Fig. 19.)

LORD'S SUPPER BANNER

Figure 19

b. When children are satisfied with their designs, they may transfer them to scrap materials. Pieces and letters should be glued carefully.
c. A dowel rod is glued to the top of the wall hanging. A piece of cord or heavy yarn can be tied to the dowel to form a hanger.

# PETER'S DENIAL

*Before the cock crows, you will deny Me three times.*
*Matthew 26:34 RSV*

## 20. Collage K—3

**Materials Needed:** construction paper, magazines, scissors and glue, black paint and brushes.

**How to Do It:**
a. Children search through magazines to find pictures illustrating how people say no to Jesus. These are cut out and glued in collage fashion to a sheet of construction paper.
b. When entire sheet of paper is covered with pictures, children write the words DO YOU SAY NO TO JESUS? over the picture with black paint.

## 21. Cock Mosaic 4—8

**Materials Needed:** heavy construction, rooster pattern (optional), glue, spaghetti, elbow macaroni, macaroni shells—large and small, spiral macaroni, scissors, wax paper, shellac.

**How to Do It:**
a. On a sheet of cardboard, children draw a rooster design. (Or you may wish to distribute the patterns shown in Fig. 20.)

COCK MOSAIC

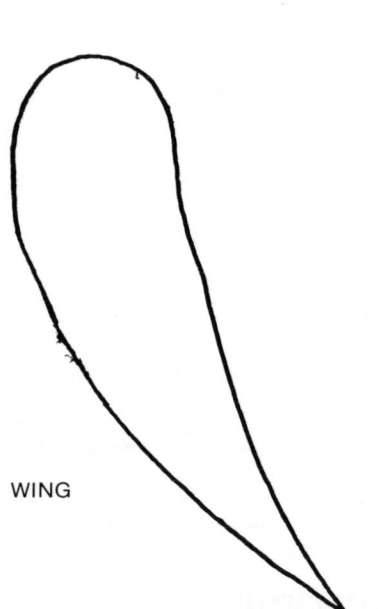

WING

To enlarge—trace on transparency, project onto large sheet of paper and trace design.

BODY

**Figure 20**

b. Shellac all pieces and glue them together on a sheet of poster board or heavy cardboard.
c. Glue macaroni in place.
   (1) NECK: small shell macaroni
   (2) BODY: large shells
   (3) WING: two layers of spaghetti
   (4) COMB & WATTLES (under beak): elbow macaroni
   (5) FEET: spiral macaroni
   (6) TAIL FEATHERS: spaghetti prepared in the following manner:

Soak the spaghetti in warm water for about 30 minutes. (Only soak a little at a time since spaghetti will get sticky and will stick together)

Cover the rooster pattern with wax paper, and place the wet spaghetti over the tail pattern. DO NOT GLUE. Dried spaghetti will remain in proper shape.

Take the wax paper off the rooster pattern and allow the spaghetti to dry overnight.

Dry spaghetti is glued to the tail pattern.

d. After the rooster is completed, children may paint with acrylics.
e. Finished rooster should be covered with several coats of shellac to preserve it.

**Variations:** pebbles, shells, dried seeds, construction paper squares, colored rice, feathers, etc. can be substituted for the macaroni.

## GOOD FRIDAY

*In the cross of Christ I glory*
*Towering o'er the wrecks of time.*
*All the light of sacred story*
*Gathers round its head sublime*
*When the woes of life o'er-take me,*
*Hopes deceive, and fears annoy,*
*Never shall the cross forsake me;*
*Lo, it glows with peace and joy!*

*John Bowring*

### 22. Match Stick Crosses K—8

**Materials Needed:** burnt wooden kitchen matches, heavy cardboard, scissors, and glue.

**How to Do It:**
a. Students first draw a cross on heavy cardboard and cut out.
b. The number of matches needed will depend on how large the cardboard base is.
c. It is advisable to burn matches *before* distributing them; this applies to the older students as well as younger. Burn the matches down below the tip and brush off excess residue before using.
d. A match base is made as in Fig. 21.

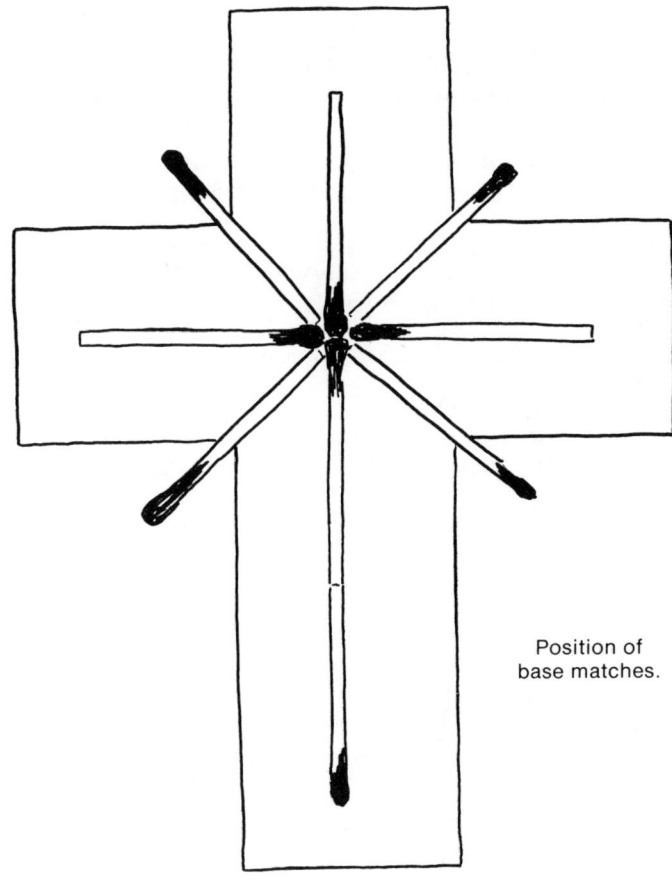

Position of base matches.

**Figure 21**

e. Matches are glued to each base match on a diagonal.
f. Matches toward the tips will need to be glued together since there will not be enough exposed cardboard to glue matches securely.
g. Finished piece is covered with one or two coats of clear shellac.
h. A hanger can be placed in the back for display purposes, or students might wish to glue entire piece onto a piece of cardboard covered with black or brown felt.

### 23. Leather Crosses K—8

**Materials Needed:** leather scraps, acrylic paints, brushes, nylon cord, and jump rings (if pendants are being made).

**How to Do It:**
a. Each student should receive a piece of scrap leather approximately 4" x 6" in size.
b. Students should experiment with various cross designs on scrap paper before transferring design to leather.
c. When design has been transferred, it is painted with acrylics, allowed to dry, and cut out. The painted cross can be covered with a thin coat of clear shellac. LET DRY COMPLETELY BEFORE USING AS BOOKMARK!
d. If children wish to make a pendant instead of a bookmark, a hole is punched into the top of each cross, and a jump ring and nylon cord are inserted.

**Variation:** K—3
If students have difficulty with drawing and cutting crosses, you may wish to give out pre-cut pieces as shown in Figure 22.

Figure 22

## 24. Quilled Crosses K—8

**Materials Needed:** quilling paper—or thin strips of lightweight white drawing paper, black construction paper, hat pins or toothpicks, glue, cardboard and scissors.

**How to Do It:**
a. Glue a piece of black construction paper to cardboard.
b. Using the basic quilling techniques shown in Figure 23, students can make various cross designs.

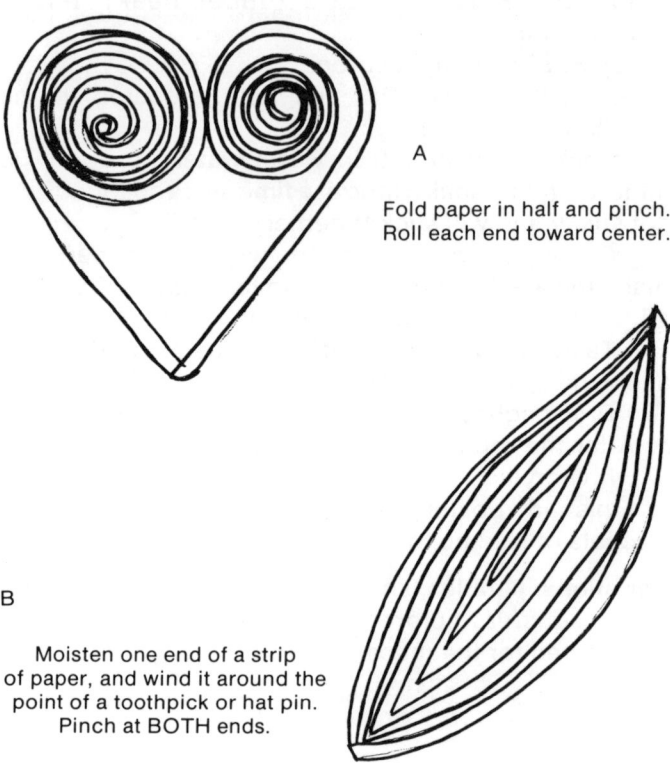

A
Fold paper in half and pinch. Roll each end toward center.

B
Moisten one end of a strip of paper, and wind it around the point of a toothpick or hat pin. Pinch at BOTH ends.

Figure 23

**Variation:** K—3
Younger students can do this as well as older children, although quilled pieces will not be wrapped as tightly. Younger, less skilled hands, might find it easier to wrap paper around pencils instead of toothpicks.

## 25. Nail Crosses K-8

**Materials Needed:** wood scraps, carpet tacks (longer nails for younger children), hammers, sandpaper, soldering irons (optional)

**How to Do It:**
a. Students should first sand the piece of wood to eliminate sharp edges and splinters.
b. An outline of a cross is drawn to cover most of the piece of wood.
c. The outline is filled in with nails hammered into the wood as close together as children can make them.

**Variation:** 4—8
If a workshop is available, older students can produce a special effect by soldering the nails together.

## 26. Egg Carton Crosses K—8

**Materials Needed:** plastic foam egg cartons, very heavy cardboard, glue, scissors, yarn, acrylics and brushes.

**How to Do It:**

a. A cross is drawn on cardboard and cut out. Paint with acrylics.
b. "Flowers" are formed by cutting out the cups and "peaks" from the foam egg cartons. (See Fig. 24a)

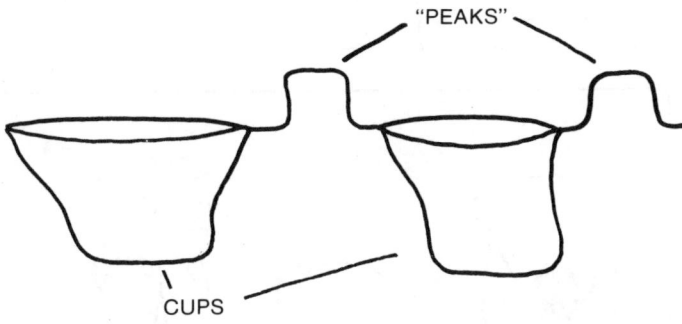

**Figure 24A**

c. Cups form the larger petals, and the "peaks" form the smaller petals. (Fig. 24B.)

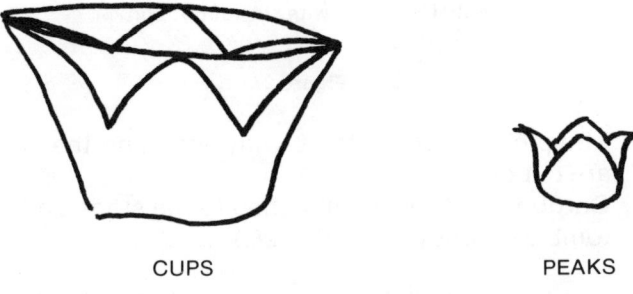

**Figure 24B**

d. The smaller "petals" are glued inside the larger "petals."
e. Flower centers are made by cutting strips of carton—½" x 1" and fringing. (See Fig. 25.) It is then rolled up and glued inside the smaller "petals."

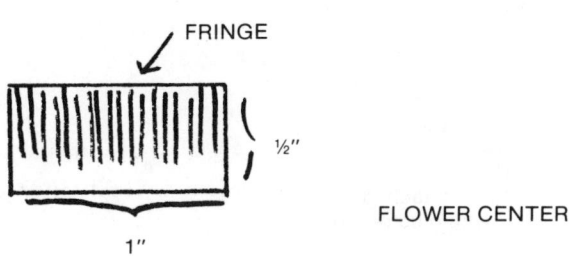

**Figure 25**

f. After flowers are painted, they are glued to the cross.
g. Leaves can be cut from the carton and painted. Glue next to flowers on cross.

# EASTER

*Why seek ye the living among the dead? He is not here, but is risen.*

Luke 24:5-6 KJV

## 27. Triptych K—8

**Materials Needed:** heavy cardboard, old Easter cards (non-secular), duplicated copy of ONE SOLITARY LIFE,* clear shellac.**

\* Here is a young man who was born in an obscure village, the child of a peasant woman. He grew up in another village. He worked in a carpenter shop until He was thirty, and then for three years He was an itinerant preacher. He never wrote a book. He never held an office. He never owned a home. He never had a family . . .

He never went to a college. He never put his foot inside a big city. He never traveled 200 miles from the place where He was born. He never did one of the things that usually accompany greatness. He has no credentials but Himself . . .

While He was still a young man, the tide of public opinion turned against Him. His friends ran away. He was turned over to His enemies. He went through a mockery of a trial. He was nailed to a cross between two thieves. While He was dying, His executioners gambled for the only piece of property He had on earth, and that was His coat. When He was dead, He was laid in a borrowed grave through the pity of a friend. Nineteen centuries have come and gone, and today He is the central figure of the human race and the leader of the column of progress. I am far within the mark when I say that all the armies that ever marched, and all the navies that ever sailed, and all the parliaments that ever sat, and all the kings that ever reigned, put together, have not affected the life of man upon this earth as has that ONE SOLITARY LIFE.

Author Unknown

\*\* A Bible verse or the seven words from the cross could be used instead.

**How to Do It:**

a. A pattern such as the one in Figure 26 is cut from cardboard.

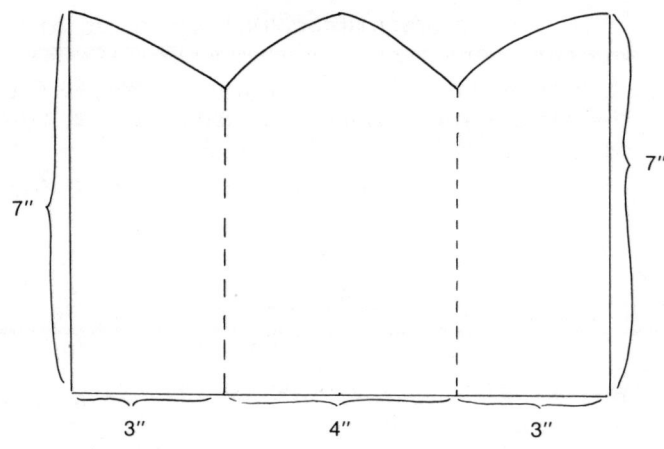

**Figure 26**

b. Paint the cardboard or laminate with colored tissue and shellac.
c. Glue Easter pictures on side panels and the piece, ONE SOLITARY LIFE (or other) on the middle panel. Laminate with clear shellac.
d. Side panels are folded toward the center panel so triptych can stand alone.

**Variation:** 4—8

Older students might enjoy making the triptych from balsa wood if materials are available. Pieces of wood would be held together with jewelry hinges.

## 28. Resurrection Picture K—8

**Materials Needed:** heavy construction paper, crayons or other coloring medium, old Easter cards, scissors and glue.

**How to Do It:**
a. Students draw pictures of tomb with body, tomb with angel, and a stone (see Figs. 27 a, b, & c). Rock and both tomb openings should be the same size so it is advisable to use a pattern for all three pictures.

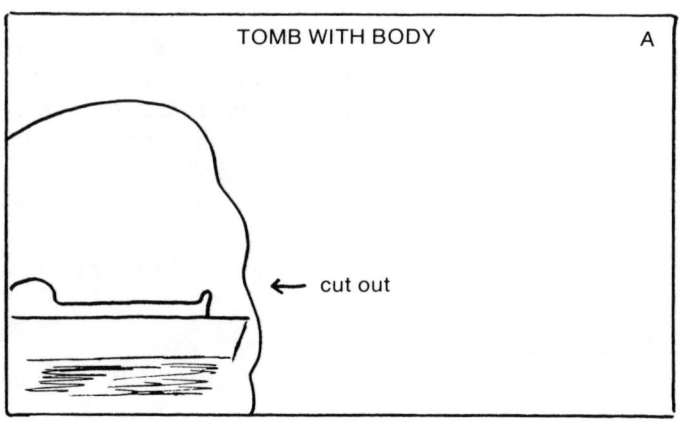

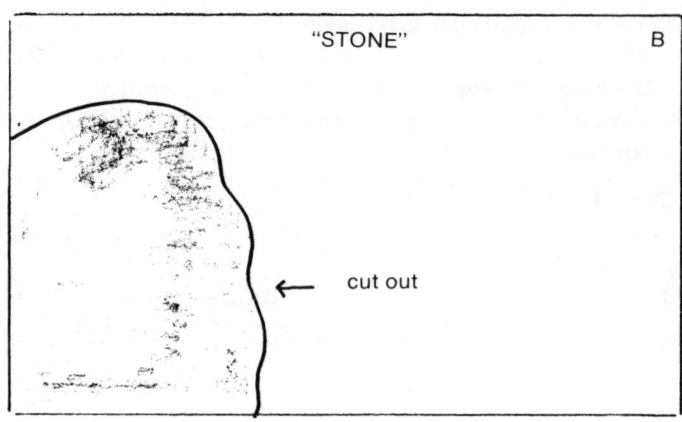

"EMPTY" TOMB    with slit cut through

**Figure 27**

b. The pictures of the tomb with body and the stone are cut out.
c. Cardboard strips are attached to the stone and the tomb with body. (See Fig. 28.)

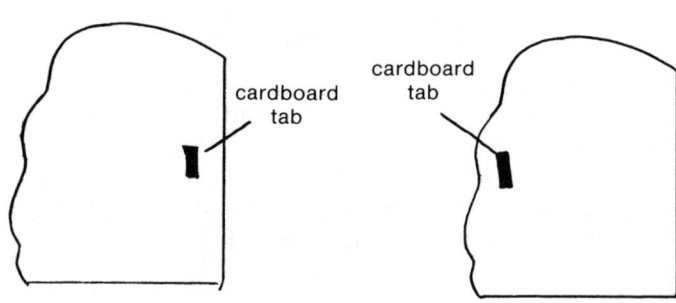

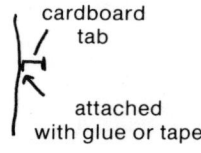

SIDE VIEW    **Figure 28**

d. A slit is carefully cut through the picture of the angel in the tomb (Fig. 27c)—leaving a 1" margin on both sides.
e. Place the tomb with the body over the angel picture—inserting the tab through the slit.
f. The rock is now inserted in the slit, and the stone is pushed in front of the tomb opening.
g. Children can now tell the Easter story by using their pictures: The covered tomb, the stone rolled away to reveal the body in the tomb, the stone rolled back and, finally, removed again to reveal the tomb with the angel.

**Variation:** *4—8*

Although this project requires some skill, older students may consider it too "childish" for them. (You could encourage them to make it for a younger friend or relative!) However, you may plan to let the older student become involved in making banners, murals, or dioramas.

## ASCENSION

*And it came to pass, while he blessed them, he was parted from them, and carried up into heaven.*

Luke 24:51 KJV

### 29. Ascension Picture K—4

**Materials Needed:** cardboard, cotton, glue, crayons or paints, heavy drawing paper or lightweight cardboard.

**How to Do It:**
a. Have children draw a background on heavy drawing paper or lightweight cardboard or tagboard. Background should include several disciples, trees, grass, etc. (See Fig. 29.)
b. On other paper or tagboard, students draw a figure of Christ and a cloud. (See Fig. 30.) Children might cut disciple and Christ figures from old Christmas and Easter cards (shepherds can double as disciples).

BACKGROUND

**Figure 29**

 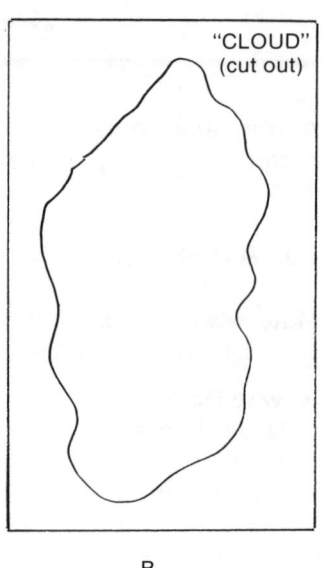

**Figure 30**

c. Cut out cloud and Christ figure. Cut slit in background picture. (See Fig. 29.) Glue tabs to Christ figure (Fig. 31).

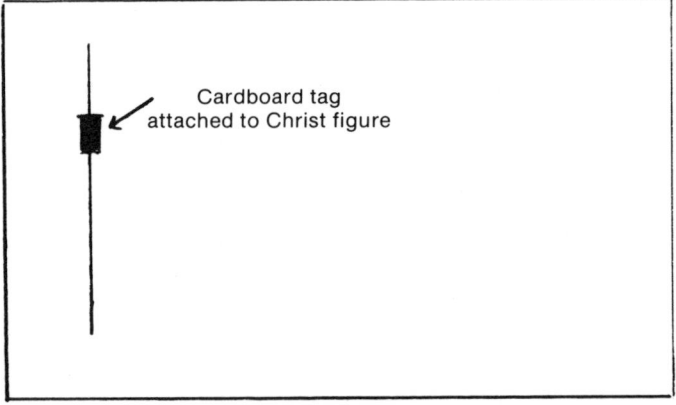

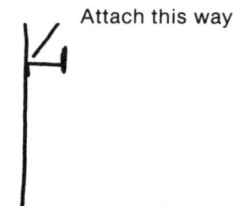

**Figure 31**

d. Glue cotton to cloud. Glue cloud over slit—putting glue only on the very edge of the back of the cloud and on the SIDES AND TOP *ONLY!* MIDDLE AND BOTTOM SHOULD *NOT* BE GLUED.

e. Christ figure is placed on picture, and the cardboard tab pushed through the slit. When the tab is pulled upward, the figure will rise upward and be hidden by the cloud.

*Go ye therefore, and teach all nations, baptizing them in the name of the Father, and of the Son, and of the Holy Ghost: Teaching them to observe all things whatsoever I have commanded you: and, lo, I am with you alway, even unto the end of the world.*
           *Matthew 28:19-20 KJV*

## 30. World Bank 5—8

**Materials Needed:** round balloons, papier mache, pins, maps of different countries, wax paper, acrylic paints, brushes, craft knives or kitchen knives, shellac.

**How to Do It:**
a. Children blow up balloons to desired size for a bank.
b. Mix instant papier mache following instructions in the appendix of this book, or use commercial instant mache which is usually more reliable.
c. Mache mix is patted over the entire surface of the balloon.
d. Mache-covered balloon should be placed on a cardboard tube section or into an empty margarine container. This should also be covered with mache and will serve as a stand for the finished bank.
e. After mache has hardened somewhat—a pin should be inserted through the mache to deflate the balloon. A coin slot can then be cut out using a craft or kitchen knife. Remove the balloon with a tweezers.
f. Students can draw countries onto the mache, or they may trace several countries onto pieces of wax paper and retrace onto mache. The traced outlines are then filled in with more mache—creating a relief map of the world.
g. When the piece is completely dry, it can be painted with acrylics and covered with a thin coat of shellac.

## 31. Church Bank 4—8

**Materials Needed:** burnt wooden matches, cardboard, glue, construction paper, shellac, masking tape.

**How to Do It:**
a. Children cut a pattern of a "building" from cardboard. (See Fig. 32.)
b. Sides are taped together with masking tape.
c. A slanting roof is also made from cardboard. It should be large enough to overlap the main building section slightly.

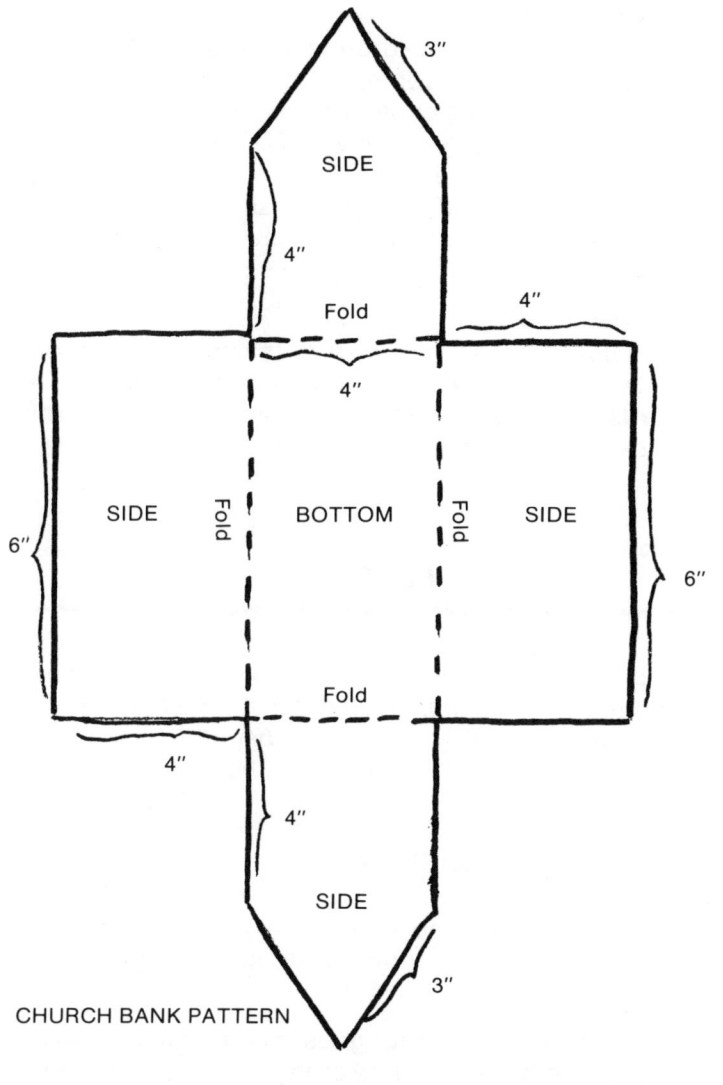

CHURCH BANK PATTERN

**Figure 32**

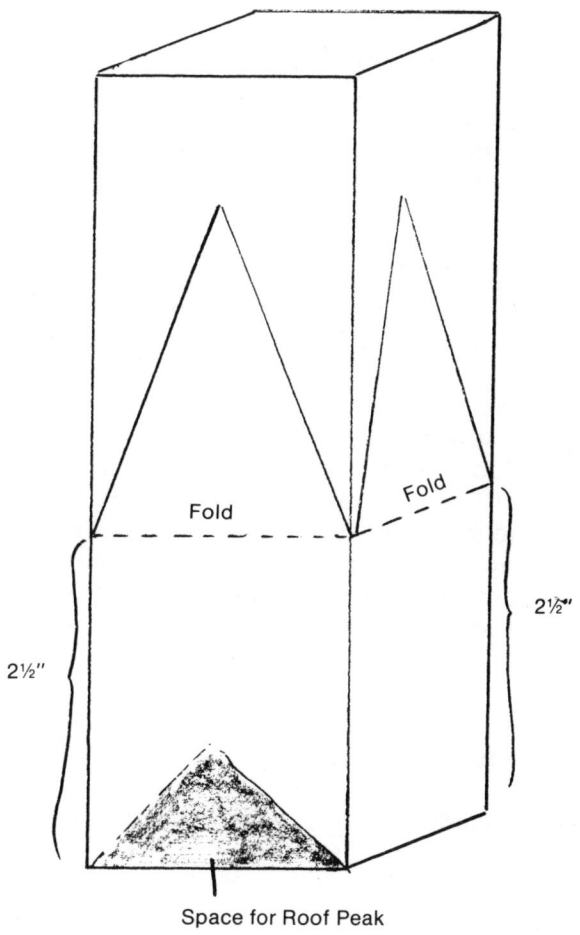

Space for Roof Peak

**Figure 33**

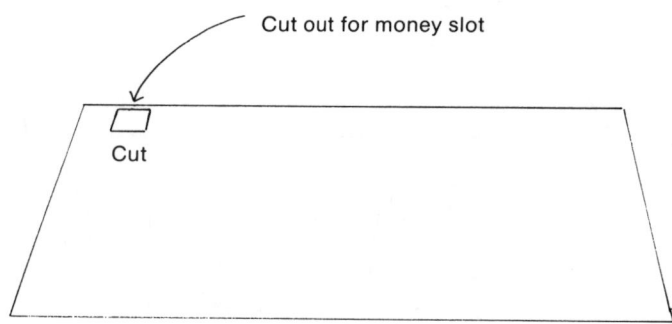

**Figure 34**

d. A bell tower can be made from a toothpaste box. (See Fig. 33.)
e. Remind children to cut two opposite sides on the bottom of the box to allow for the roof peak.
f. All pieces should be fitted together BUT NOT GLUED! Any necessary adjustments should be made at this time. When all pieces fit together properly, children should lightly trace around the base of the bell tower so the pattern shows on the roof.
g. In one section of this pattern, children should cut a hole large enough so money can be taken out as well as put in. This hole will later be covered by the bell tower (Fig. 34).
h. Children are now ready to attach matches. Building *base* should be done first. Matches are glued horizontally—peaked sections are done vertically.
i. Attach the roof with heavy glue. Matches are attached to the roof in a vertical position. Remind students *not* to cover the patterns they traced onto the roof earlier.
j. The bell tower is covered with matches while it is separate from the rest of the building.
k. The finished tower rests on the roof—it is *not* attached.
l. Doors and windows can be made from construction paper and added to the church.

**Variation:** *K—3*
**Materials Needed:** cardboard, pattern, glue, paints, toothpicks, and construction paper.

**How to Do It:**

a. Give each child the building pattern shown in Figure 32.
b. Children cut the pattern out, glue it on the cardboard, and cut out again. A roof should also be made at this time.
c. Pieces are folded and glued together.
d. A slot is cut at the top of the roof.
e. Children can paint structure as desired.
f. A simple cross can be made by gluing two toothpicks together and gluing them to the front of the roof.
g. Windows and doors are made from construction paper and attached.*

* The door can also serve as a way to get the money out. BEFORE gluing the base together, children should cut out the top, side, and bottom of the door. Insert a winged paper fastener from the *inside* so "wings" are showing outside. These will serve as a door "latch" and keep the door closed securely.

## 32. Baptism Banner K—8

**Materials Needed:** felt and other material scraps, glue, scissors, dowel rods, yarn.

BAPTISM BANNER

Figure 35

**How to Do It:**

a. Give children a background material piece approximately 12" x 18" (or larger, if desired).
b. Using felt scraps or other material, students cut out various symbols illustrative of Baptism (Dove, cross, Baptismal Font, etc.).
c. Child's name and date of Baptism can be placed on the banner as a reminder of New Life (Fig. 35).
d. Attach a dowel rod and tie on yarn for hanger.

**Variation:** 4—8

Older children might enjoy making a banner of a butterfly—using various bright-colored yarns. The words BAPTISM—NEW LIFE can be formed from black felt and attached with glue.

## PENTECOST

*And there appeared unto them cloven tongues like as of fire, and it sat upon each of them. And they were all filled with the Holy Ghost and began to speak with other tongues, as the Spirit gave them utterance.*
Acts 2:3-4 KJV

## 33. Tongues of Fire K—8

**Materials Needed:** red, orange and yellow construction paper, heavy thread, dowel rods, scissors, glue.

**How to Do It:**

a. Children make 12 "tongues" of fire from each of the three colors—12 red, 12 orange, 12 yellow. (See Fig. 36.)

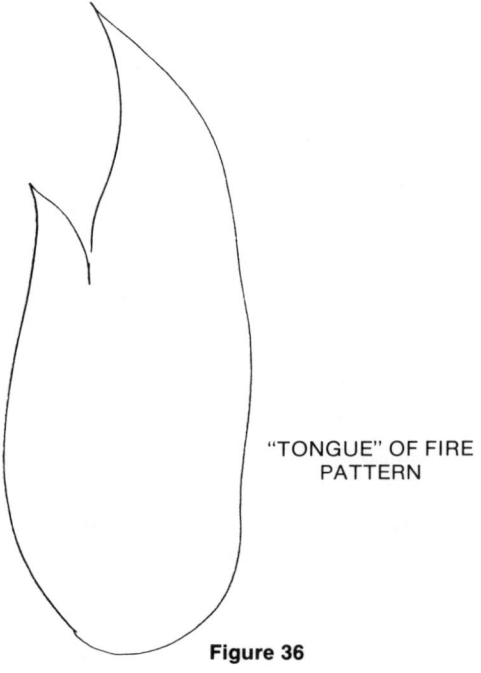

"TONGUE" OF FIRE PATTERN

Figure 36

b. Tongues are glued together in sets of three colors so all three colors show. They are then attached to heavy thread.
c. Let children experiment with lengths of thread and position to get a suitable arrangement for their mobiles.
d. The name of Christ can be written in a different language on each of the tongues before hanging.

**Variation:** *4—8*

Other possibilities for older children might be banners, murals, dioramas.

K—3—Younger children might put on a puppet show.

# Chapter 2: Other Holidays

## THANKSGIVING

*Make a joyful noise unto the Lord, all ye lands. Serve the Lord with gladness; come before His presence with singing. Know ye that the Lord He is God; it is He that hath made us and not we ourselves; we are His people, and the sheep of His pasture. Enter into His gates with thanksgiving, and into His courts with praise; be thankful unto Him and bless His name. For the Lord is good; His mercy is everlasting; and His truth endureth to all generations.*

*Psalm 100 KJV*

### 34. Collage 4—8

**Materials Needed:** cardboard, magazines, glue, scissors, "onion skin" typing paper, shellac.

**How to Do It:**
a. Students cut out pictures which illustrate things for which we should thank God. (They may wish to include photos of family members, special friends, or even a favorite pet.)
b. When cardboard is completely covered with pictures, a thin coat of clear shellac should be applied.
c. Using felt-tipped pens, students copy a prayer or Bible verse onto a half sheet of onion skin. (This can be ironed with a warm iron to simulate aging parchment.)
d. "Parchment" is rolled up once and released.
e. Two opposite corners of the "parchment" are attached to the collage with glue (Fig. 37).

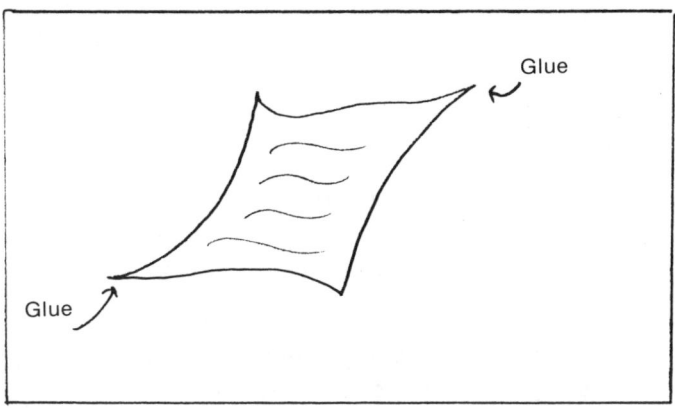

THANKSGIVING COLLAGE         Figure 37

### 35. Thanksgiving Booklets K—3

**Materials Needed:** construction paper, magazines, scissors, glue, several prayers duplicated by the teacher, hole puncher, yarn.

**How to Do It:**
a. Each child should receive at least five sheets of construction paper.
b. Punch two holes in each sheet. (Be sure holes are lined up properly.)
c. Children cut out pictures illustrating things for which they are thankful. Pictures are glued carefully to the inside pages. (Children may wish to design a cover using crayons or paints.)
d. Give out duplicated prayers, and let children cut them apart and glue one to each page of the booklet. (Read each prayer, and let children decide which picture to use with each.)
e. Booklets are tied together with yarn.

### 36. Table Mats K—8

**Materials Needed:** heavy cardboard, magazines, construction paper in fall colors, clear contac paper, glue, scissors.***

**How to Do It:**
a. Children cover the cardboard with pictures illustrative of the season OR with an abstract design made from construction paper. (You might suggest leaf and fruit designs.)
b. A Thanksgiving prayer is glued to the center of the design.
c. Entire piece is covered with a sheet of clear, self-adhesive plastic.

***If time and materials permit, you may wish to allow children to make a set of four mats to be used at home.

### 37. Thanksgiving Posters K—8

**Materials Needed:** tagboard or 12" x 18" construction paper, poster colors or crayons, brushes, scissors, glue, newspapers, water for cleanup.

**How to Do It:**

a. Students should choose a slogan of no more than six words (Father, we thank Thee; Give Thanks to the Lord; The Lord is a great God, etc.).
b. Students paint pictures illustrative of the season.
c. When the picture is dry, the slogan is printed over it. Letters should be large enough to see from a distance.
d. To preserve posters, you may wish to allow children to cover them with a clear coat of shellac.

## MOTHER'S DAY

*Honor thy father and thy mother: that thy days may be long upon the land which the Lord thy God giveth thee.*
*Exodus 20:12 KJV*

### 38. Dried Flower Holder K—8

**Materials Needed:** scrap wood, paint or felt-tipped pens, dried flowers OR handmade flowers, drills (either hand or electric) with ¼" bit, sandpaper, clear shellac.**

**How to Do It:**

a. Wood scraps are sanded to eliminate sharp areas and splinters.
b. A ¼" hole is drilled in the tops of the wood scraps. Holes should be approximately ¾" deep.
c. The wood can be painted or left in its natural state and covered with several coats of clear shellac.
d. Using paint or a felt-tipped pen, children write the Bible verse—"Consider the lilies of the field, how they grow"—or another appropriate verse can be chosen.

e. Dried or handmade flowers are inserted into the hole at the top of the wood (Fig. 38).

**\*\*K—3** For younger children, holes should be drilled into wood scraps before project time. Also—since motor skills may not have developed sufficiently in younger children, you may wish to duplicate a Bible verse which can be cut out and glued to the front of the wood.

### 39. Flowers and Vase K—3

**Materials Needed:** 9" x 12" construction paper, colored tissue paper, scissors, glue, compasses.

**How to Do It:**

a. Using compasses, children make a construction paper circle at least 8" in diameter.
b. The circle is cut out and a slit is cut from one end to the center. (See Fig. 39.)

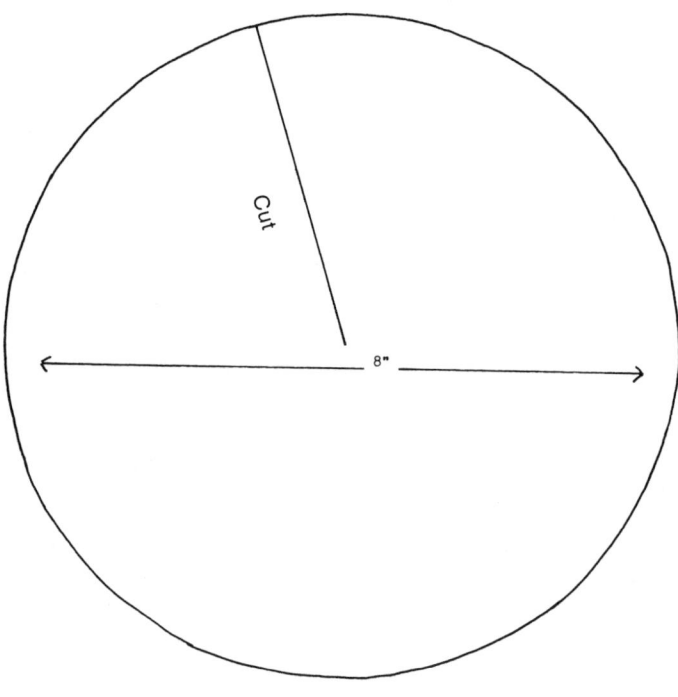

**Figure 39**

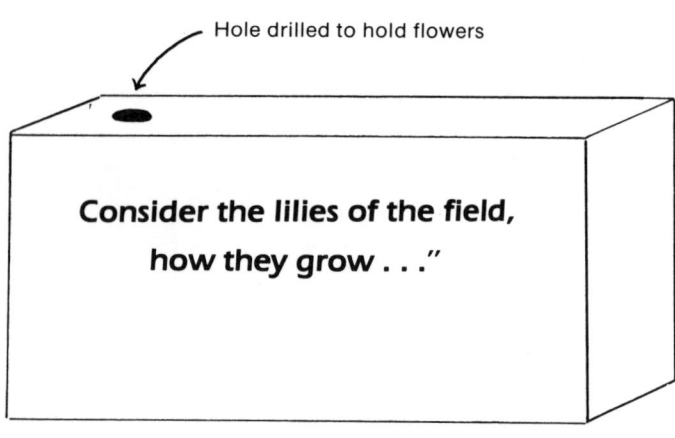

**Figure 38**

c. The circle is pulled together to form a cone "vase." This is glued at the seam (Fig. 40).
d. Cone may be filled with dried flowers or with handmade flowers sprayed with a light cologne.

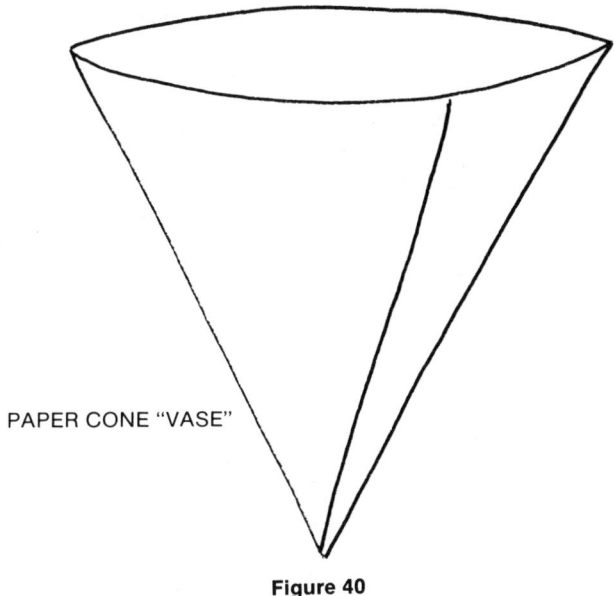

**Figure 40**

PAPER CONE "VASE"

CONNECTED CARDBOARD FRAME

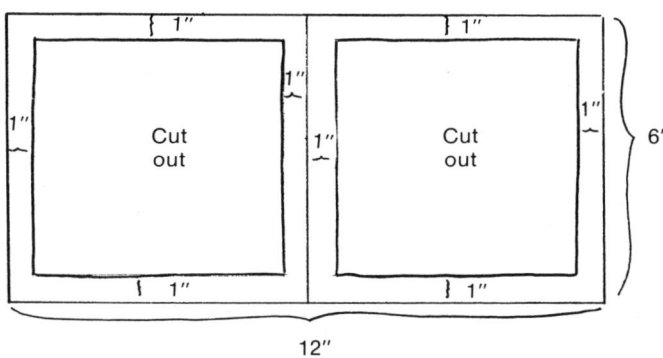

**Figure 41**

### 40. Mothers Are God's Special People 4—8

**Materials Needed:** cardboard, wax paper, dried leaves or flowers, felt-tipped pens, shellac, glue, paint, colored tissue, scissors.

a. Students first make two connecting frames and two separate frames as shown in Figures 41 and 42.
b. Paint one side of each frame.
c. Children receive 4 sheets of wax paper—each 6" x 6."
d. Two sheets of wax paper are coated with an even, heavy layer of clear shellac.
e. On one of the pieces of wax paper, students place the dried leaves and flowers, pressing firmly and working out the air bubbles.
f. The back of each item is dabbed with a bit of shellac.
g. A piece of colored tissue is placed over the dried leaves arrangement *and* on the blank sheet of shellacked wax paper.
h. Air bubbles should be worked out at once.
i. A thin layer of clear shellac is CAREFULLY brushed over both pieces.
j. The other two pieces of wax paper are used to form two "sandwiches"—one with dried flowers and the other with only a piece of colored tissue. Air bubbles should be removed once again.
k. Allow both wax paper "sandwiches" to dry completely.
l. On the FRONT of the plain wax paper "sandwich" students write the phrase—MOTHERS ARE GOD'S SPECIAL PEOPLE—with a felt-tipped pen or black paint. This should be allowed to dry.
m. The larger frame is folded slightly so it will stand by itself—painted side on the BACK.

SEPARATED CARDBOARD FRAMES

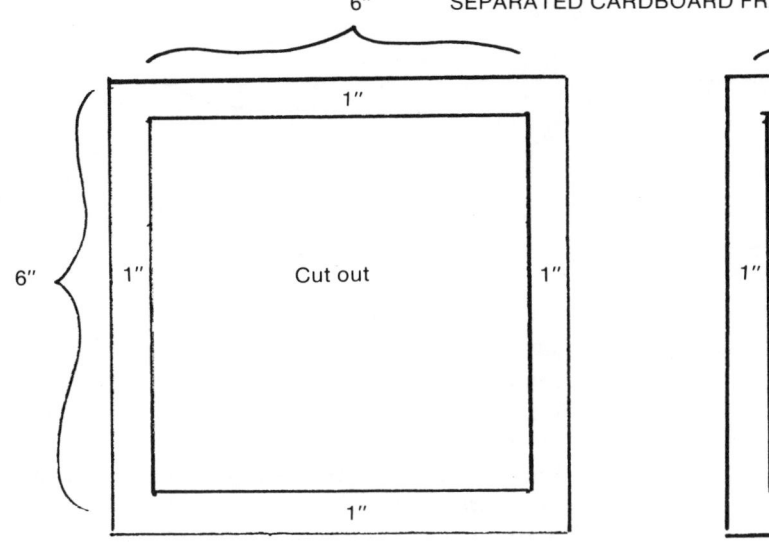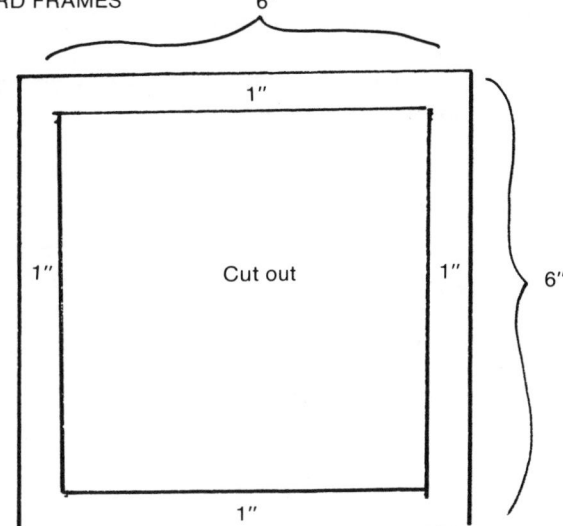

**Figure 42**

n. The wax paper pieces are glued to the inside of the frame—one piece on each side.
o. The two single frames are glued—painted side up—over the larger frame to form a cardboard "sandwich." The windows will now have a verse and a picture showing through.

## 41. Wall Hangings K—3

**Materials Needed:** cardboard, yarn or ribbon, material scraps, old birthday cards, scissors, glue.

**How to Do It:**
a. Children cut out a geometric design from cardboard.
b. Cardboard figure is covered with material and allowed to dry.
c. Pictures of flowers or animals are cut from old greeting cards and glued onto the material.
d. The outside of the figures are trimmed with yarn or ribbon.
e. A hangar can be made from yarn or ribbon and glued to the back.
f. OPTIONAL: Children may like to copy a Bible verse onto the hangings using felt markers (GOD IS LOVE; LOVE ONE ANOTHER, etc.).

## FATHER'S DAY

## 42. Personality Plaque 3—6

**Materials Needed:** wood scraps, felt and other material scraps, picture wire, tacks, scissors, glue, sandpaper.

**How to Do It:**
a. Wood scraps are sanded to eliminate sharp edges and splinters.
b. A piece of wire is tacked to the back of the wood to serve as a hanger. (See Fig. 43.)

BACK OF WOOD SCRAP

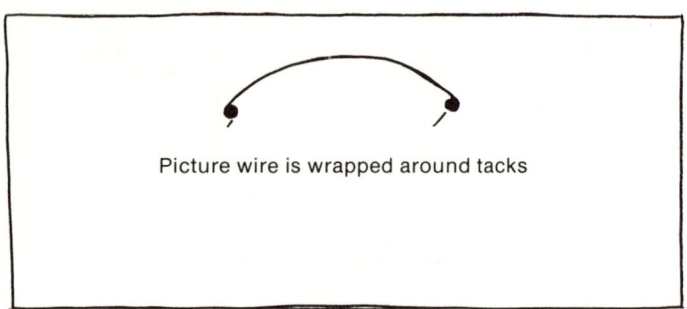

Picture wire is wrapped around tacks

**Figure 43**

c. Wood can be painted or left in its natural state and covered with a thin coat of shellac.
d. Words describing the child's father are cut from felt or other material. (Words can describe personalities, favorite foods, or pastimes, etc.) These are glued, with the word FATHER, to the wood scraps. Words should be different sizes and glued vertically and horizontally.

## 43. Fear Not, I Will Pilot Thee K—8

**Materials Needed:** craft sticks, cardboard, glue, small paper cups, acrylic paints, brushes, scissors, compasses.

**How to Do It:**
a. Children draw a circle—7" in diameter—from cardboard and cut out.
b. Leaving a 1" border, the center of the circle is cut out. (See Fig. 44.)

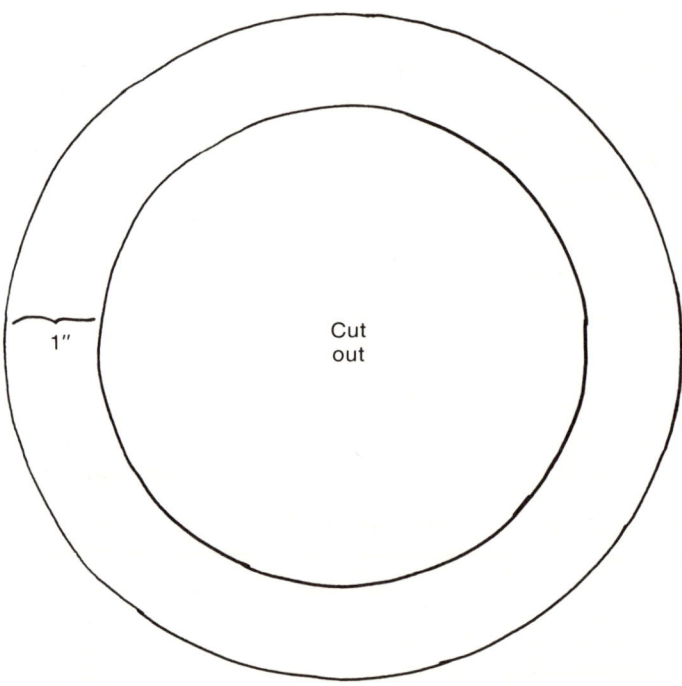

**Figure 44**

c. Circles are painted to simulate wood.
d. Each child paints 8 craft sticks.
e. A 12" x 18" piece of heavy cardboard is painted a different color.
f. When paint is dry, the circle is glued to the center of the cardboard.
g. Craft sticks are glued to the circle as shown in Figure 45.

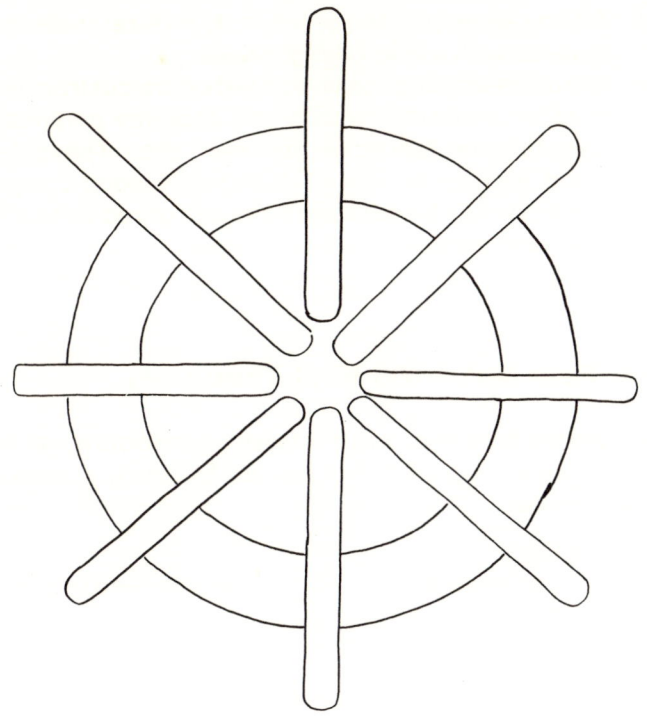

**Figure 45**

k. With felt-tipped markers or paints, the words—FEAR NOT, I WILL PILOT THEE—are written at the top of the cardboard. Attach a hanger to the back.
l. Fathers (or another male relative) can now use this as a convenient bulletin board—attaching notes to each spoke of the wheel with tacks.

## 44. Paper Weight K—8

**Materials Needed:** large smooth rocks, white base coat paint, brushes, glue, nature pictures, shellac.

**How to Do It:**
a. Rocks are painted with base coat—one side at a time.
b. Nature scenes are cut from magazines or old greeting cards and glued to one side of the work.
c. Several coats of clear shellac are applied—allowing each coat to dry completely before applying another.

**Variations:**
a. Rocks may be left in their natural state. A thin coat of shellac is applied and allowed to dry. Follow steps 2 and 3 above.
b. Students may prefer to paint a design directly onto the rock. This is allowed to dry and several coats of shellac are applied.

h. Using white paint, names of days of the week are written on each stick—leaving the top stick blank.
i. A paper cup is cut in half and the outside painted. This will serve as the "hub" of the wheel.
j. The "hub" is glued upside down to the center of the circle and craft sticks (Fig. 46).

**Figure 46**

# Chapter 3: The Old Testament

## CREATION

*In the beginning, God created the heaven and the earth.*

*Genesis 1:1 KJV*

### 45. Laminations K—8

**Materials Needed:** ordinary wax paper, clear shellac, brushes, leaves and dried flowers (or students can draw items representing creation), colored tissue.

**How to Do It:**
a. Students cut two pieces of wax paper to the size they want for their laminations (9" x 12" usually works best).
b. One piece of wax paper is coated with an even, heavy layer of clear shellac.
c. Objects or pictures which are to be laminated are placed FACE DOWN in the shellac. Students should press down firmly and work out air bubbles.
d. The back of each item is dabbed with a bit of shellac.
e. A piece of colored tissue or cellophane is laid over the arrangement to add a bit of color. (This stage is optional.) Air bubbles should be worked out once again.
f. Students should now CAREFULLY brush on a layer of clear shellac.
g. The second piece of wax paper is carefully added and sealed firmly—again working out air bubbles which may have formed between layers.
h. Allow to dry before hanging.

**Variation:** K—3

Since young children and sticky shellac don't always go well together, you may wish to let children iron the two pieces of wax paper together. A warm iron will melt the wax and this will serve as an adhesive for the two pieces.

### 46. Creation Banner K—8

**Materials Needed:** felt or other material scraps, glue, 9" x 12" pieces of felt, scissors, large plain sheet.

**How to Do It:**
a. Give each student a piece of 9" x 12" felt and place other material scraps in a central location.
b. Each student will make a small "banner" illustrating something that God created. (See Fig. 47.)

Figure 47

c. When separate pieces are completed, they can be attached to an old sheet with one or two stitches or with staples and hung from a curtain rod or dowel rod. When you are ready to remove the display, each child can take his/her piece home as an individual banner.

*Now the serpent was more subtle than any beast of the field which the Lord God had made.*

*Genesis 3:1 KJV*

## 48. Serpent Puppet K—3

**Materials Needed:** large paper plates, green material scraps, green socks (from home), construction paper, scissors, paint, glue.

**How to Do It:**
a. The inside of the plate is painted; allow to dry.
b. Plate is folded in half—painted side on the *inside*.

## 47. Tissue Paper Collage K—8

**Materials Needed:** tagboard, flat brushes, white glue mixed with water (½ and ½), clean rags or paper towels, colored tissue in *light* colors (dark colors will appear black when overlapped).

**How to Do It:**
a. Encourage the children to work out a design on scrap paper first. Remind them that each object will be cut out SEPARATELY and glued onto the board.
b. TEARING AND CUTTING: Objects which have rough surfaces (trees, mountains, clouds, etc.) should be *torn* from tissue. Objects with smooth surfaces (people, certain animals, fruits) should be cut with scissors.
c. GLUING PROCESS: Once students have decided upon a picture, each separate piece of tissue is applied in the same manner.
(1) The area on the tagboard which will be covered by a particular piece is marked off LIGHTLY in pencil.
(2) Glue is brushed onto the tagboard in this area.
(3) The tissue piece is CAREFULLY lowered onto the glued surface.
(4) Glue is then brushed over the surface of the paper to coat it—removing air bubbles at the same time. SMALL WRINKLES SHOULD NOT BE REMOVED! These add texture and—when children try to remove them—tissue usually tears.
d. When the picture is completed and dry, the entire piece is covered with a thin layer of the glue mixture.
e. Pictures may tend to bend while drying. WHEN COMPLETELY DRY they can be placed under heavy weights to flatten.

**Variation:** K—3 Tissue paper may be hard to handle for younger children. Construction paper may be substituted for the tissue.

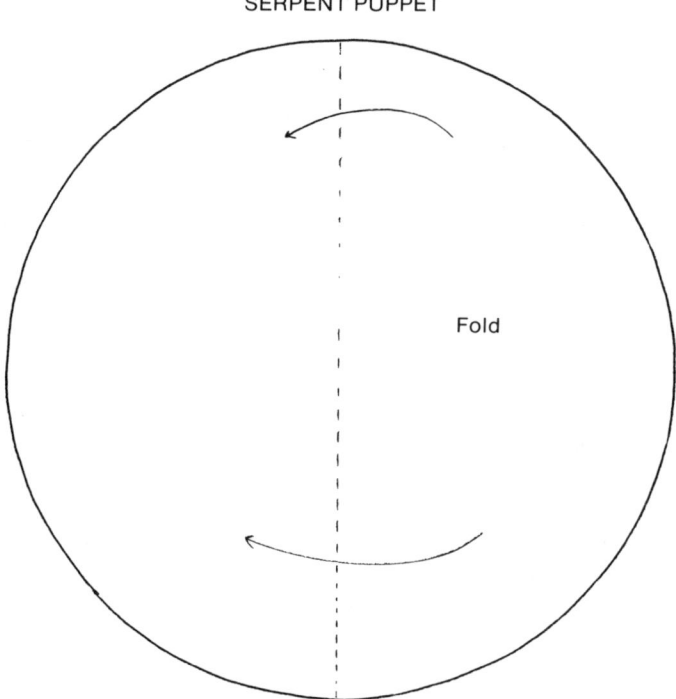

Paint inside of plate and fold

**Figure 48**

c. A piece of green cloth is glued or stapled to the top half of the plate—leaving room for fingers.
d. Have children place their fingers in the cloth section and mark off a line where their thumbs cover the bottom half of the plate.
e. A small cut is made in the bottom half for a thumb hold.
f. From construction paper, teeth, tongue, and eyes are made and glued to the head.
g. A body can be made from a green sock. A thumb hole should be cut out of the sock.

## NOAH

*And God said unto Noah, The end of all flesh is come before Me; for the earth is filled with violence through them, and, behold, I will destroy them with the earth. Make thee an ark of gopher wood; rooms shalt thou make in the ark, and shalt pitch it within and without with pitch.*

*Genesis 6:13-14 KJV*

### 49. Noah's Ark Plaque *K—8*

**Materials Needed:** heavy cardboard, bread dough mixture, glue, scissors, acrylics.

**How to Do It:**

a. Children draw (or you may wish to duplicate) patterns similar to those in Figures 49, 50, and 51.

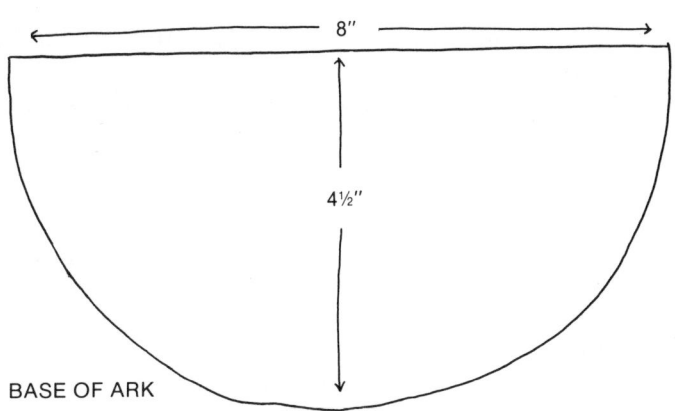

BASE OF ARK

**Figure 49**

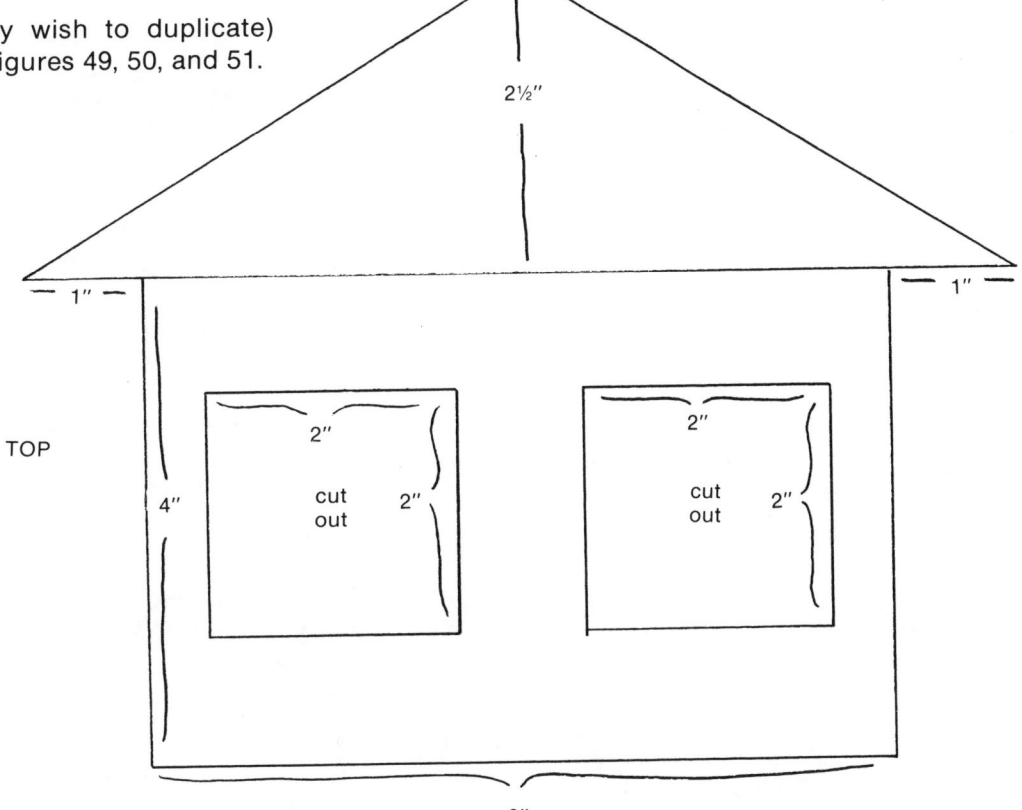

ARK TOP

**Figure 50**

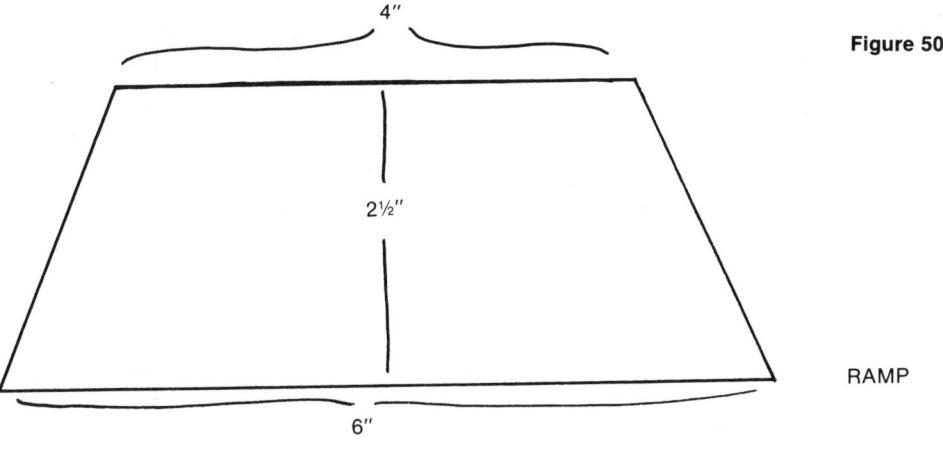

RAMP

**Figure 51**

b. Patterns are cut out, transferred to cardboard, and cut out again.
c. Four cardboard strips are glued to the *back* of the ark base. (See Fig. 52.)
d. All three ark pieces are painted with acrylics and allowed to dry.
e. Mix several batches of bread dough and, while children are waiting for paint to dry, they may make several sets of animals from the dough. (See Figs. 53 & 54.) These patterns are merely suggestions. Children should be encouraged to create their own animals. Give them directions for FLAT dough pieces.

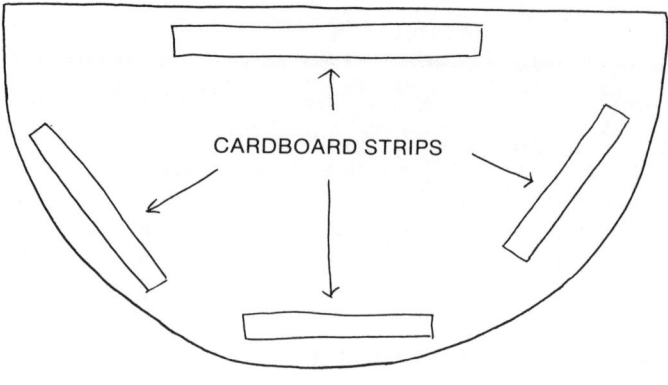

BACK OF ARK BASE

**Figure 52**

Place head in "window."

Use broom bristles for whiskers.

← Place on ramp.

Trace basic pattern onto flattened piece of bread dough and cut out. Features are painted on after bread dough cools. "Hair" can be made from yarn.

**Figure 53**

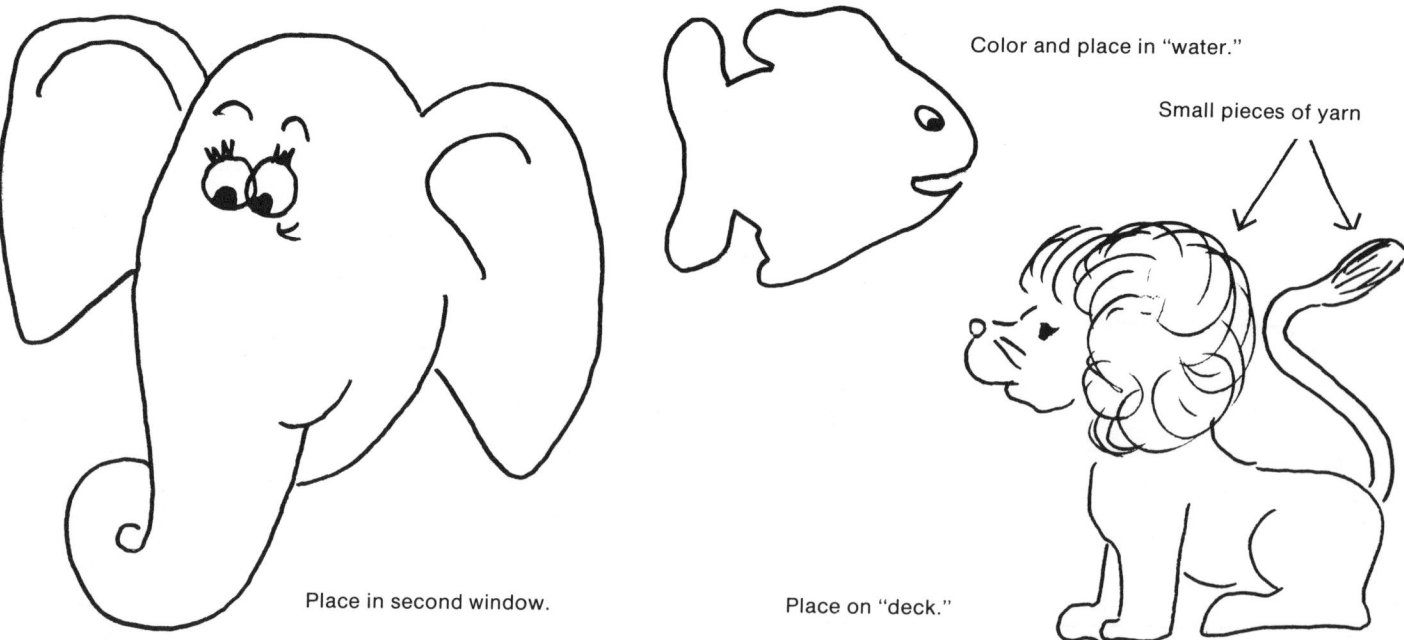

Place in second window.

Color and place in "water."

Small pieces of yarn

Place on "deck."

**Figure 54**

f. ARK TOP is glued to the background piece.
g. Glue animal heads to windows.
h. Glue ARK BASE into position. Glue animals to the "deck" just below the raised edge of the base.
i. RAMP is glued to base.
j. Animals are glued to the ramp.
k. Finished picture may be covered with a coat of clear shellac.

## 50. Ark Model 5—8

**Materials Needed:** cardboard, glue, masking tape, craft sticks, pipe cleaners, heavy construction paper, yarn, acrylic paints, milk containers, scissors, or single-edge razor blades.

**How to Do It:**
a. Students make cardboard sections similar to those shown in Figures 55 and 56. (Size will depend on materials and time available.)

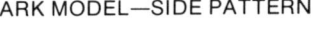
ARK MODEL—SIDE PATTERN

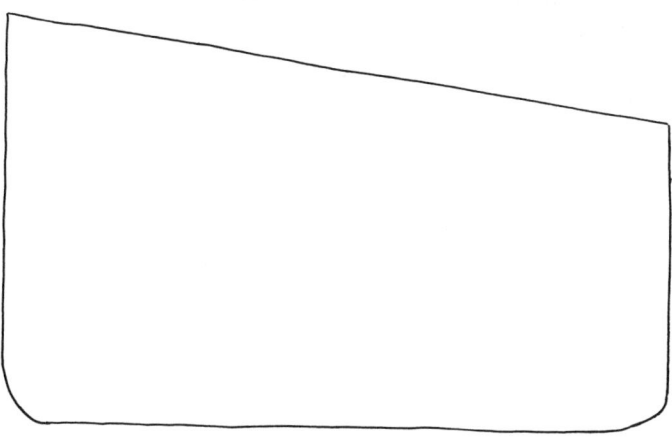
Make two of equal size.

**Figure 55**

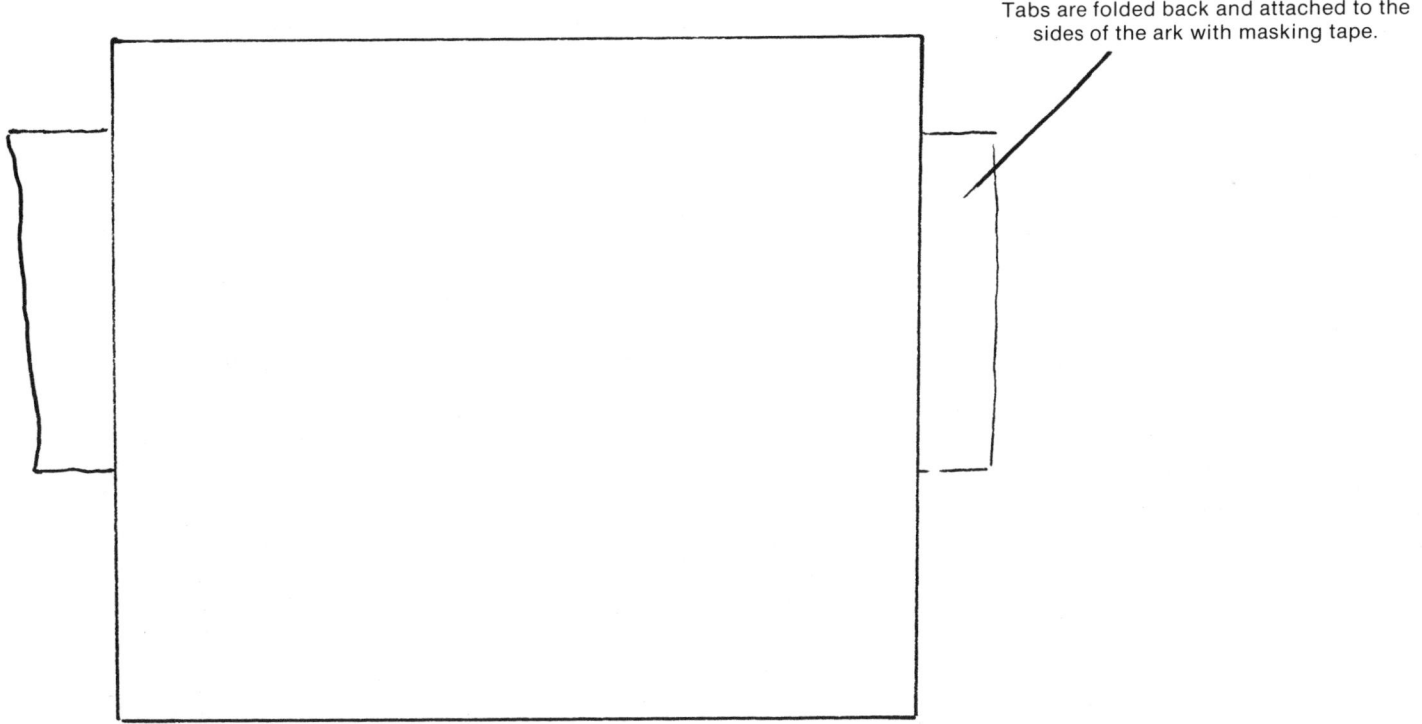

Tabs are folded back and attached to the sides of the ark with masking tape.

Back section should be slightly lower than front section to fit tapered sides.

**Figure 56**

b. The top of a milk container serves as the "cabin." (Quart size for small arks, larger sizes for larger arks.)
c. Before attaching the front and back sections to the sides, craft sticks are glued about ¼" below the INSIDE top edge of each piece. (See Fig. 57.) These will hold the deck securely to the ark.

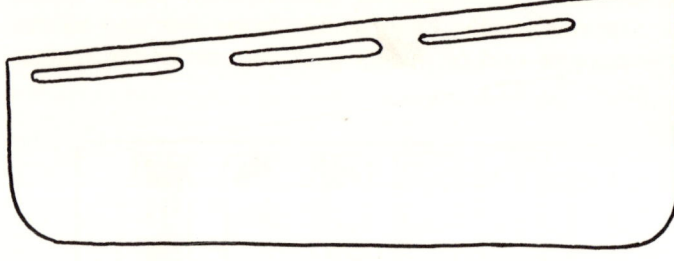

SIDE 1

BACK AND FRONT

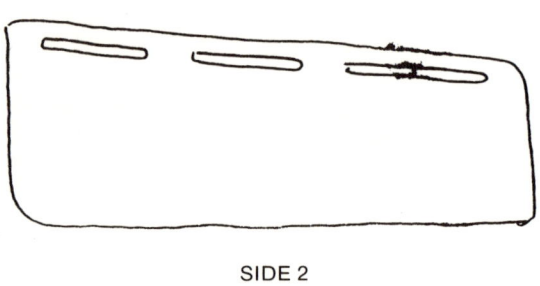

SIDE 2

**Figure 57**

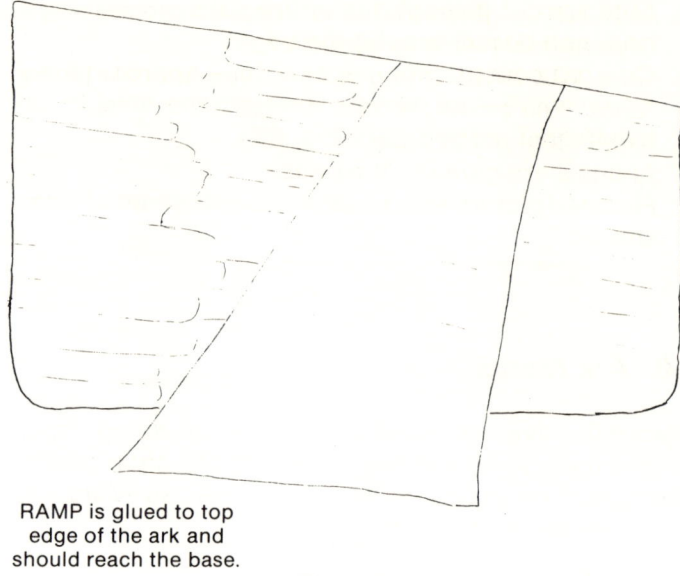

RAMP is glued to top edge of the ark and should reach the base.

**Figure 58**

## JOSEPH

*Now Israel loved Joseph more than all his children because he was the son of his old age; and he made him a coat of many colors.*

*Genesis 37:3 KJV*

### 51. Coat of Many Colors K—3

**Materials Needed:** heavy construction paper, scissors, glue.

**How to Do It:**
a. Children draw (or you may wish to duplicate) a coat pattern similar to the one in Fig. 59.

d. A "deck" is made from cardboard to fit snugly against the sides of the ark.
e. When all cardboard sections have been glued or taped together, students cover the outside with craft sticks glued horizontally (OR they may use burnt matches, papier mache or just paint with acrylics.)
f. Cover the milk container top with the same material used for the base. This is then glued to the deck.
g. A ramp is made from cardboard, glued to the top edge of one of the sides and covered with the same type of material used to cover the other pieces (Fig. 58).
h. If paper mache is used to cover the cardboard base, students should paint as desired. If craft sticks or burnt matches were used, students can coat with several thin layers of clear shellac.
i. Animals can be made from craft sticks, pipe cleaners, bread dough mixture, or other medium.

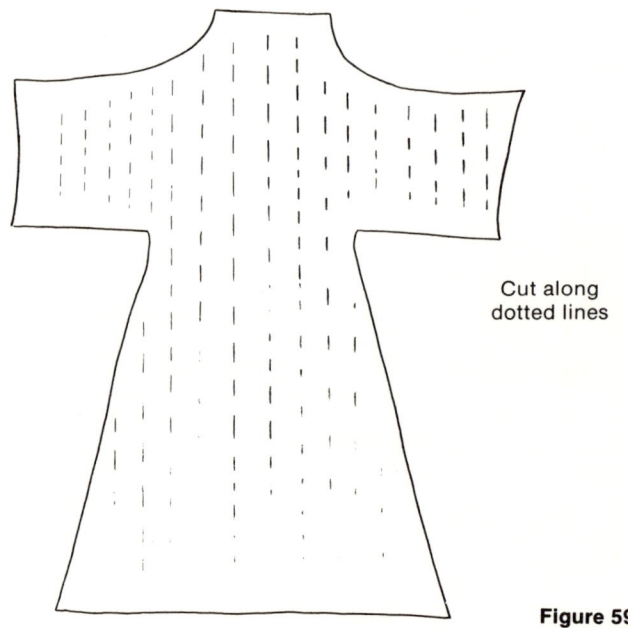

Cut along dotted lines

**Figure 59**

b. Slits are cut through the entire pattern—leaving a one-inch border around the edges.
c. Colored construction paper strips—approximately 1" in width—are woven through the slits in an over/under motion. (See Fig. 60.)

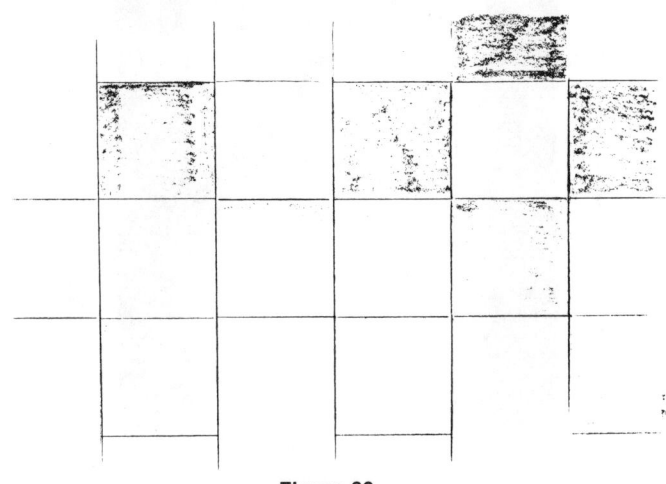

**Figure 60**

d. Strips can be secured at the back of the picture with glue or tape.

**Variation:**

**Materials Needed:** cardboard, duplicated coat pattern, colored construction paper, scissors, glue.

**How to Do It:**
a. Children make a cardboard frame—cutting out the inside of a piece of 8½" x 11" piece of cardboard and leaving a 1" border (Fig. 61).

**Figure 61**

b. Children glue colored construction paper strips (approximately 1" in width) from one end to the opposite end of the longest section of the frame. (See Fig. 62.)

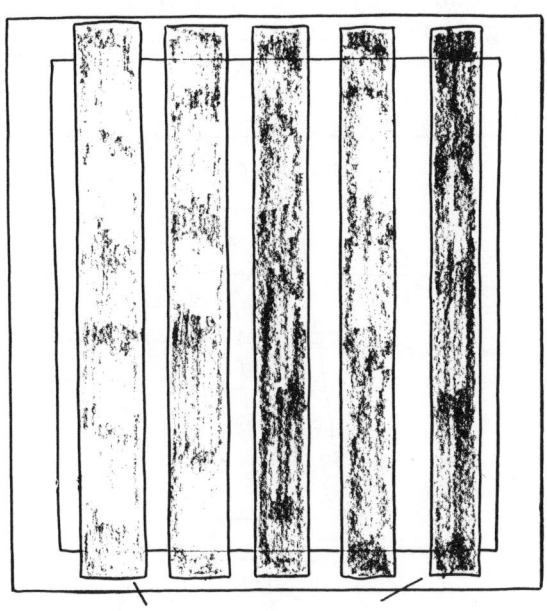

Strips are glued in place.

**Figure 62**

c. Construction paper strips are now woven in an over/under pattern across the loom.
d. Give students a duplicated coat pattern as in Fig. 63.

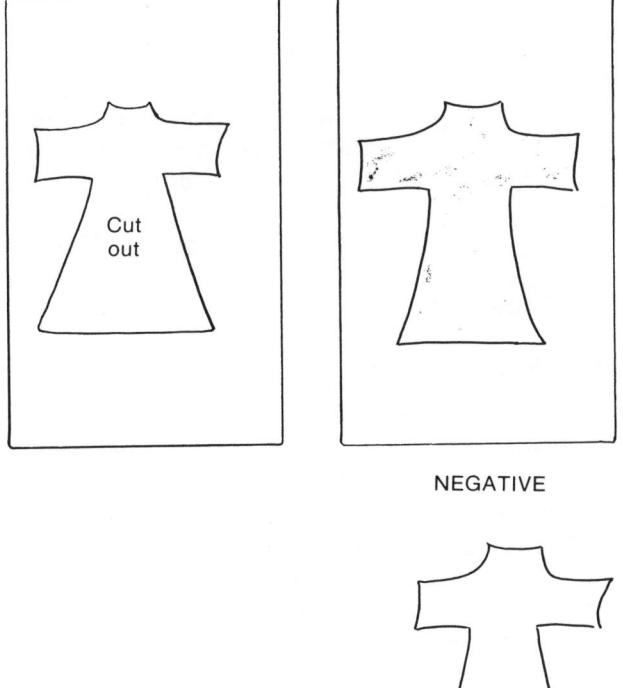

**Figure 63**

NEGATIVE

POSITIVE

e. WITHOUT cutting through the border of the pattern, the coat is cut out. The NEGATIVE pattern is used. (See Fig. 63.)
f. The sheet with the negative coat pattern is glued to the cardboard frame. The woven pattern will show through the coat. (See Fig. 64.)

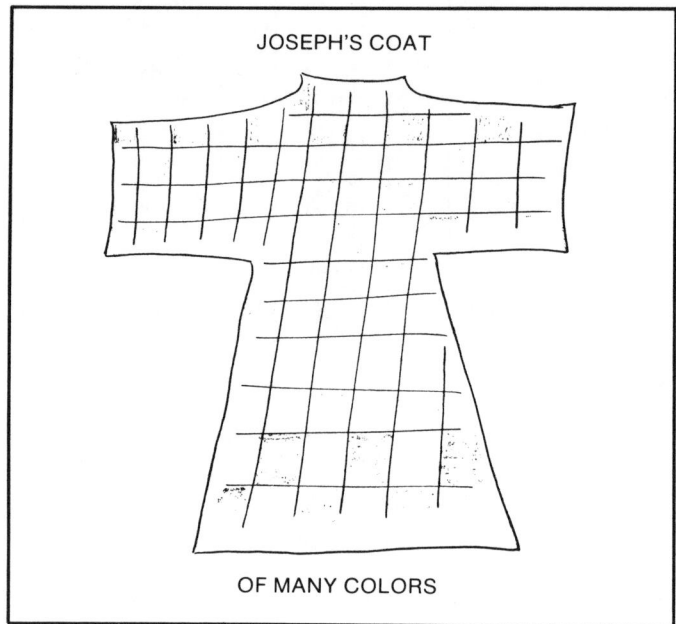

**Figure 64**

*Now the sons of Jacob were twelve . . . Reuben . . . Simeon . . . Levi . . . Judah . . . Issachar . . . Zebulun . . . Joseph . . . Benjamin . . . Dan . . . Naphtali . . . Gad . . . Asher. . . .*

*Genesis 35:22-26 KJV*

## 52. Logos 4—8

**Materials Needed:** newsprint, tagboard, acrylics, brushes.

**How to Do It:** Logos are visual symbols which identify a product or person to the public. The dove, for example, is a logo for the Holy Spirit; ☧ is a logo for Christ.
a. Using newsprint, students make various sketches for the names of Jacob's sons—using various types of lettering. Letters may be elongated, exaggerated, distorted, and placed in an interesting design.
b. When students are pleased with a particular sketch, it can be enlarged and transferred to a sheet of tagboard. The final design should be developed in one color, in black, or in a combination of black and a color (Fig. 65).

**Figure 65**

## 53. Circle "Movie" 4—8

**Materials Needed:** large sheets of tagboard, winged paper fasteners, acrylic paints or other coloring media, scissors, or single-edge razors.

**How to Do It:**
a. Two large circles of equal size are cut from tagboard.
b. One tagboard circle is marked off into "pie" sections of equal size. The number of sections will depend on the number of scenes to be depicted.
c. The second circle has one "pie" section cut out—shown in Fig. 66.

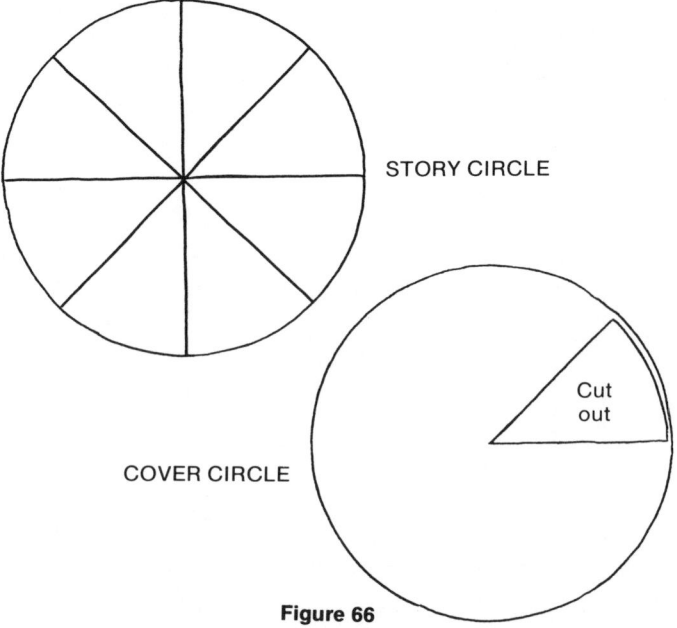

**Figure 66**

d. A scene depicting an aspect of Joseph's life is drawn into each "pie" section. (Scenes should be in correct order.)
e. After the scenes are completed, the two circles are fastened together with a paper fastener.
f. Attach a piece of cardboard to the *back* of the story circle. This will allow students to move the circle more easily.

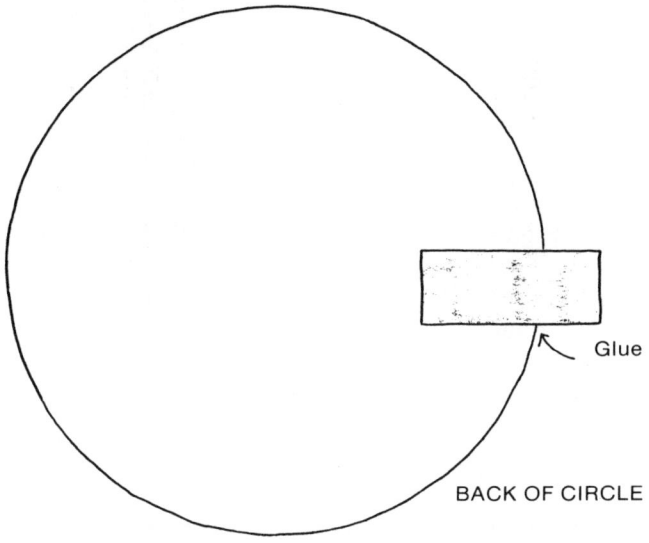

**Figure 67**

**Variation:** *K—3*
Although many younger children are capable of doing this project on an individual basis, you may wish to use this as a group project.
a. Give each child a piece of paper the size of a "pie" section in the circle.
b. Each child depicts a given scene.
c. Completed scenes are glued—in sequence—to a large tagboard circle on the bulletin board.
d. Story circle is covered with a cover circle (as in Fig. 66).

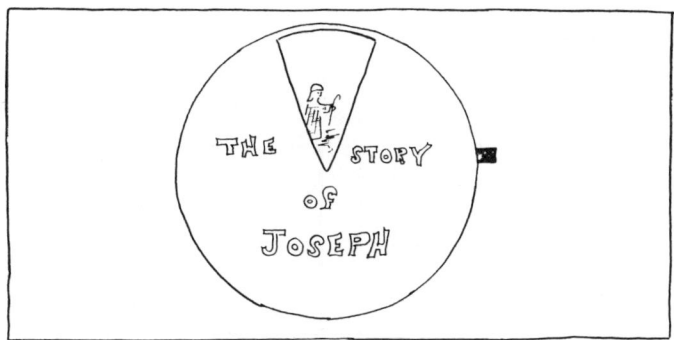

**Figure 68**

# MOSES

*And when she could no longer hide him, she took for him an ark of bulrushes and daubed it with slime and with pitch and put the child therein.*

Exodus 2:3 KJV

## 54. Reed Basket *4—8*

**Materials Needed:** molds (grocery boxes, roasting pans, etc.), newspaper, wheat paste, scissors, paper toweling.

**How to Do It:**
a. Work area should be covered with newspaper for easy cleanup.
b. Turn the mold upside down.
c. Measure from one rim, up the side, across the bottom, and down the other side to the opposite rim. (See Fig. 69.)

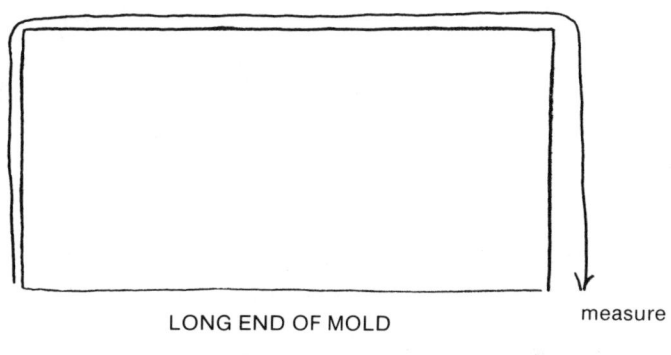

LONG END OF MOLD

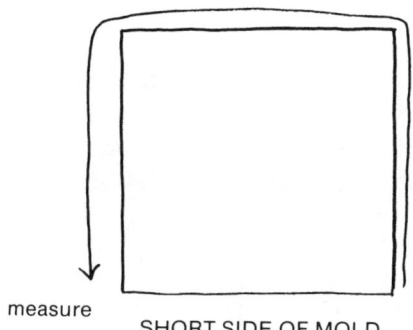

SHORT SIDE OF MOLD

**Figure 69**

This distance will determine the length of the longest strips needed for the project.

d. Cut enough lengths of newspaper to avoid having to stop in the middle of the project. Strips should be between ½" and 1" in width. Variety in size will make the basket more interesting.
e. Strips are dipped into water to dampen. Strips are removed, and wheat paste mixture is applied with fingers. Excess paste should be removed.

f. Strips are laid across the sides and top of the mold—first lengthways, then across the width (Figs. 70 & 71).

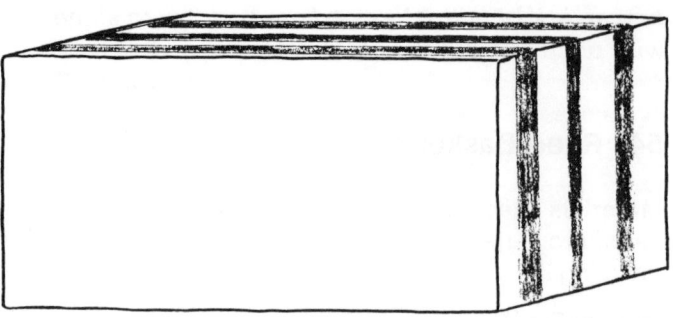

**Figure 70**

**Figure 71**

g. Several sheets of paper toweling are dipped into water, then wheat paste. Squeeze out excess paste, and spread towels over the top of the mold to seal all holes. SIDES SHOULD NOT BE COVERED!

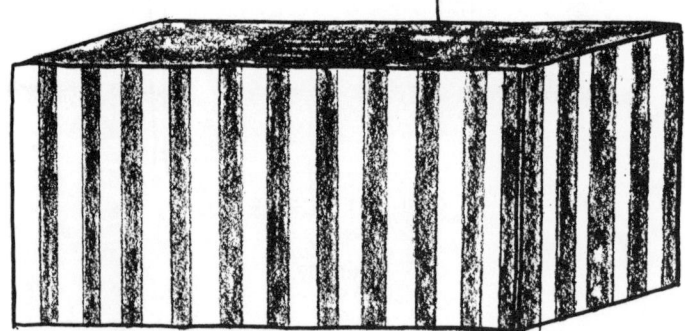

**Figure 72**

h. Strips of newspaper (dipped in paste) are woven over and under the other strips. This should be a continuous pattern around the mold. These strips should be as close to each other as possible. Be sure each strip ends INSIDE the basket before finishing. (See Fig. 73.)

Begin weaving at top.

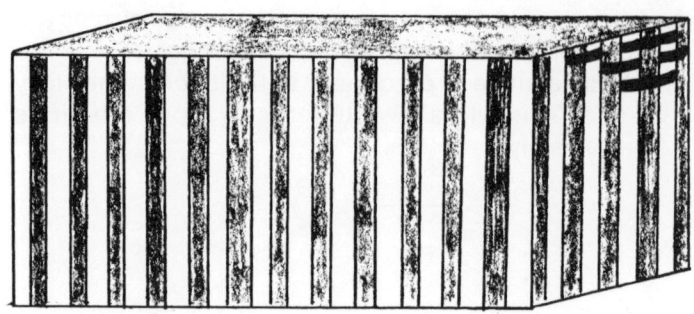

**Figure 73**

i. The woven basket should dry ON THE MOLD, or it will collapse. After it is COMPLETELY dry, the basket can be removed and painted or covered with several coats of shellac.

j. Baskets will be sturdy enough to use for storage.

**Variation:** *K—3*

a. Give children the pattern similar to the one shown in Fig. 74.

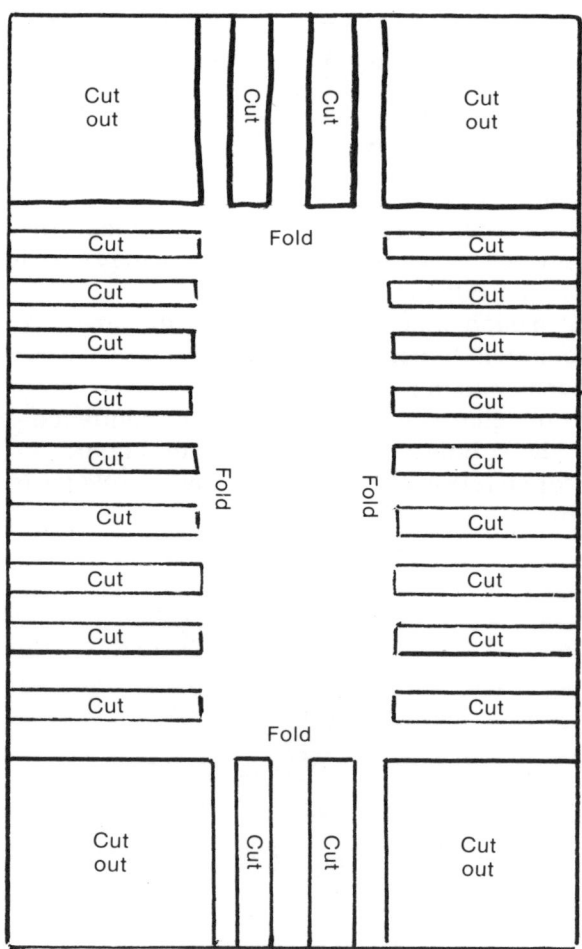

**Figure 74**

b. Using strips of colored construction paper, students weave through the upright strips in an over/under pattern. Glue to secure.

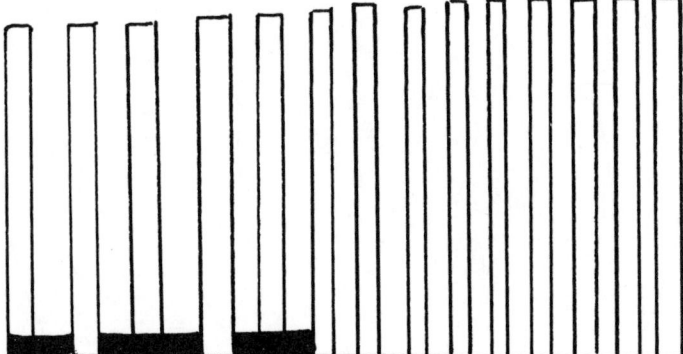

Begin weaving from the bottom

**Figure 75**

*And the angel of the Lord appeared unto him in a flame of fire out of the midst of a bush.*

Exodus 3:2 RSV

## 55. The Burning Bush K—4

**Materials Needed:** heavy drawing paper, colored tissue or cellophane, glue, scissors, paint or crayons, tagboard, paper fasteners.

**How to Do It:**
a. Students draw (or you may wish to duplicate) a picture of Moses caring for the sheep at the mount. (See Fig. 76.)
b. Children should also draw and cut out a circle approximately 6 inches in diameter. (Center should be marked.)
c. A bush is drawn on opposite sides of the circle as in Fig. 77.

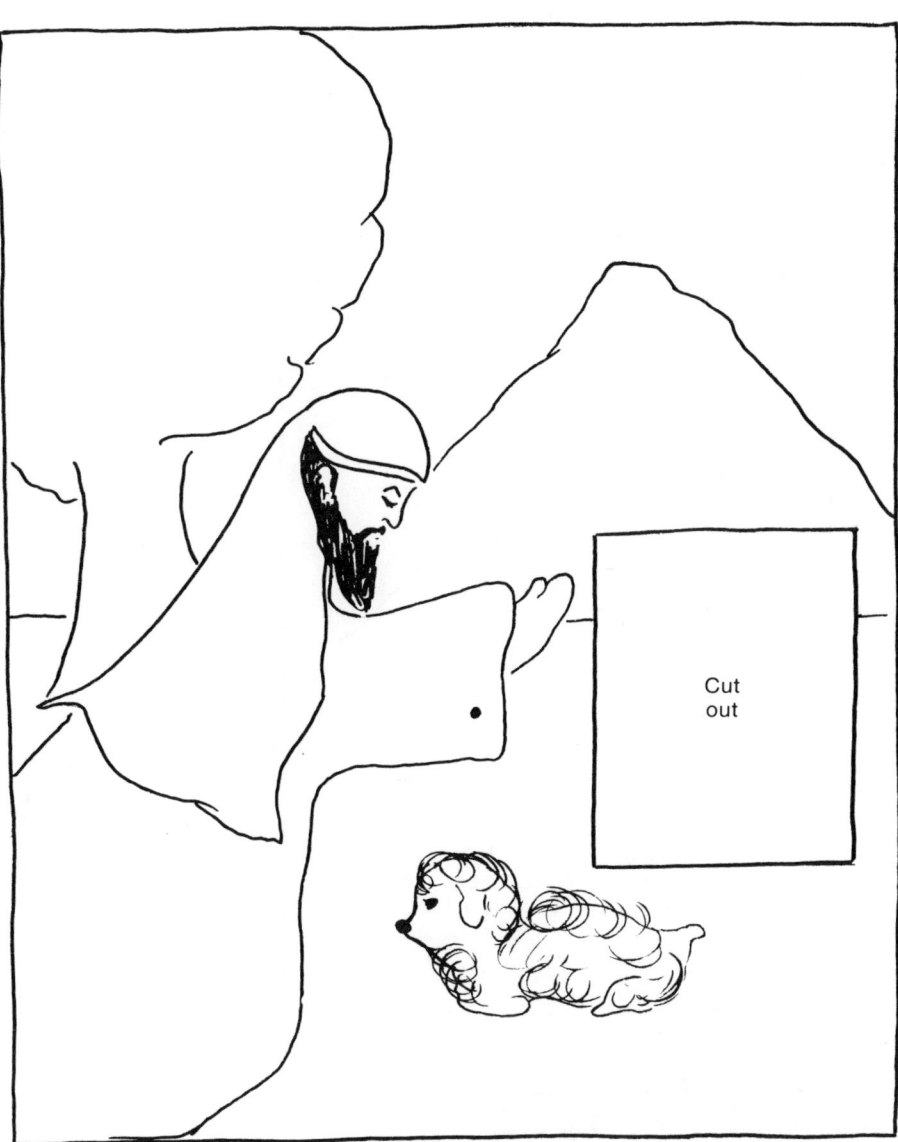

**Figure 76**

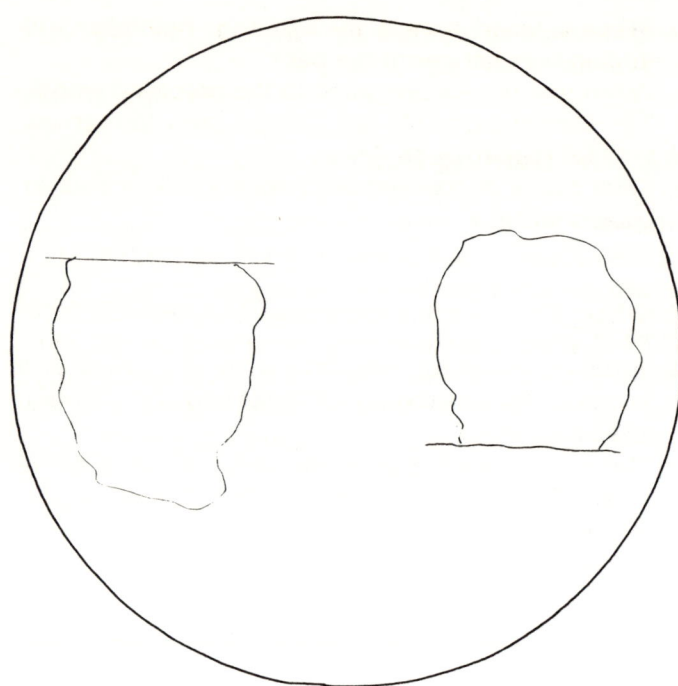

**Figure 77**

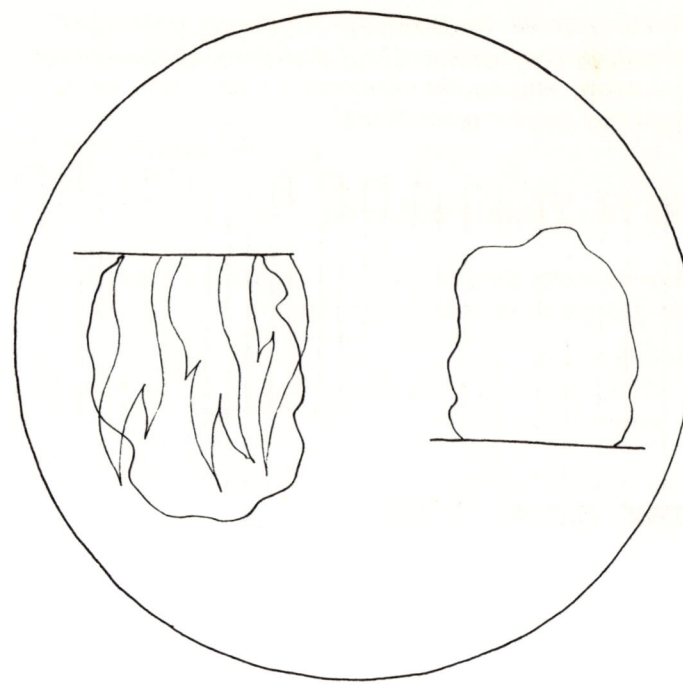

**Figure 78**

d. From colored tissue or cellophane, children cut out "flames" and glue to ONE of the bushes. (See Fig. 78.)

e. Attach the circle to the back of the picture with a winged paper fastener. The bushes will show through as the wheel is turned (Figs. 79 A & B).

**Figure 79A**

**Figure 79B**

50

*And the Lord said unto Moses, Come up to Me into the mount, and be there: and I will give thee tables of stone, and a law, and commandments which I have written; that thou mayest teach them.*

*Exodus 24:12 KJV*

## 56. The Tablets of Stone K—2

**Materials Needed:** cardboard, duplicated sheet of the Ten Commandments, tablet pattern.

**How to Do It:**
a. Children trace tablet pattern (Fig. 80) onto cardboard and cut out.

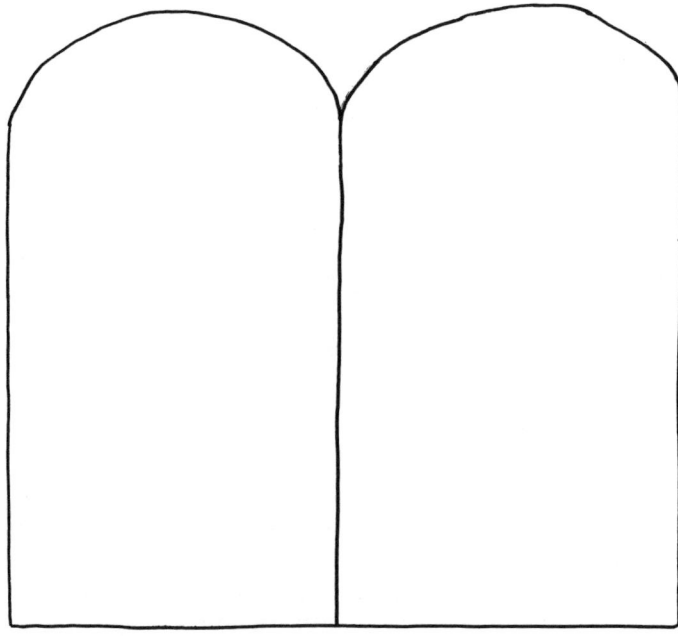

**Figure 80**

b. The Ten Commandments are glued to the cardboard tablets.
c. Place yarn or wire on back for hanger.

**Variation:** If time permits, mix a batch of baker's clay and give each child a flat piece. Tablet pattern is traced onto the baker's clay. Excess is pulled away, and "tablets" are baked according to directions. When the "tablets" are cool, children may glue the Ten Commandments to them and laminate with ½ water/½ glue mixture or with clear shellac.

### The Tablets of Stone 3—8

**Materials Needed:** papier mache mash (commercial), paint or felt-tipped pens, wood scraps, shellac.

**How to Do It:**
a. Students form two "stone tablets" from the mache mash. Allow to dry completely.
b. Prepare wood scraps by sanding, painting, and adding wire hanger to the back.
c. When dry, tablets are glued to the prepared wood.
d. Ten Commandments are printed onto the tablets with felt-tipped pens.
e. Final piece is covered with several thin coats of clear shellac.

**Variation:** There is a product known as KARVASTONE which can be purchased from most craft stores. This can be placed in an aluminum foil mold, allowed to dry, and the Ten Commandments carved directly onto the tablets using a stylus or other sharp instrument.

# DAVID

*And David put his hand in his bag, and took thence a stone, and slang it, and smote the Philistine in his forehead, that the stone sunk into his forehead, and he fell upon his face to the earth.*

*1 Samuel 17:49 KJV*

## 57. David and Goliath K—4

**Materials Needed:** tagboard, crayons or paints, scissors, glue, or tape.

**How to Do It:**
a. Instruct students to draw a picture of David and background scenery on a 9" x 12" sheet of tagboard.
b. Two slits should be cut into the picture as in Fig. 81.
c. Goliath and a stone are drawn on other paper or cardboard and cut out.

**Figure 81**

d. Cardboard tabs are taped to the back of the two pieces. (See Fig. 82.)

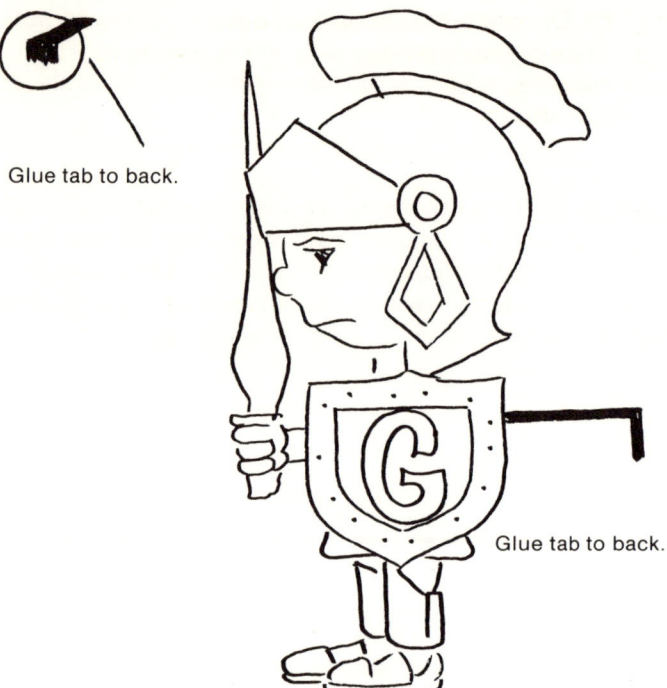

**Figure 82**

e. Slip the tab stone through the upper slit, the tab on Goliath through the bottom slit (Fig. 83).

**Figure 83**

f. Children can move the stone and hit Goliath. The figure of Goliath will then "fall" to the ground (Fig. 84).

Goliath "Falls"

**Figure 84**

## 58. David and Goliath Flip-It Book 4—6

**Materials Needed:** drawing paper, paint or other medium, staples.

**How to Do It:**
a. Drawing paper should be cut into 5" x 7" pieces for easy handling.
b. Each child should receive at least 10 sheets of paper.
c. Students sketch out the confrontation between David and Goliath in 10 or more consecutive steps. Each picture should show a slight progression of movement (stone getting closer, Goliath's sword being raised, etc.).
d. When the students are satisfied with their preliminary sketches, they may transfer the sketches to the booklet pages and color them in. Pages should be numbered consecutively.
e. Finished booklets are stapled together—page one on the BOTTOM and so forth. When booklets are "flipped," they will show movement in correct order.

**Variation:** 7—8 Animated films can be made quite easily using developed, UNUSED 8mm or 16mm film and fine-line markers.

Divide the blank film among the group. Develop a simple "script," and assign each student a particular movement to transfer to the film. Since film frames are rather small, fine-line markers are best for the job.

Have someone splice the finished pieces together and show to the class. Dialog and background music might be added by using a tape recorder.

*And it came to pass, when the evil spirit from God was upon Saul, that David took an harp, and played with his hand.*

*1 Samuel 16:23 KJV*

## 59. David's "Kinnor" K—8

**Materials Needed:** 4—8 dowel rods, cardboard, papier mache, old guitar strings or rubber bands of different sizes and widths.

**How to Do It:**

a. Duplicate and distribute the patterns shown in Figs. 85 and 86.

b. Students cut out and trace both patterns onto cardboard—Figure 85 TWICE, Figure 86 FOUR TIMES.

c. Cardboard patterns are cut out.

d. Tape or glue the base (Fig. 85) at the top fold ONLY. (See Fig. 87.)

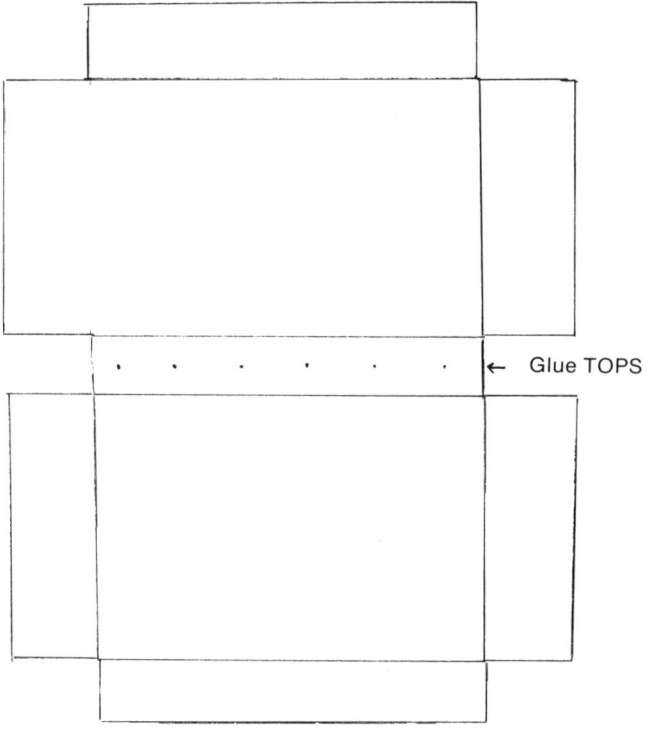

**Figure 87**

e. String the guitar strings or rubber bands through the holes, securing them under the flap.

f. The rest of the base is now glued together. Tops are glued together and glued or taped to the base. (See Fig. 88.)

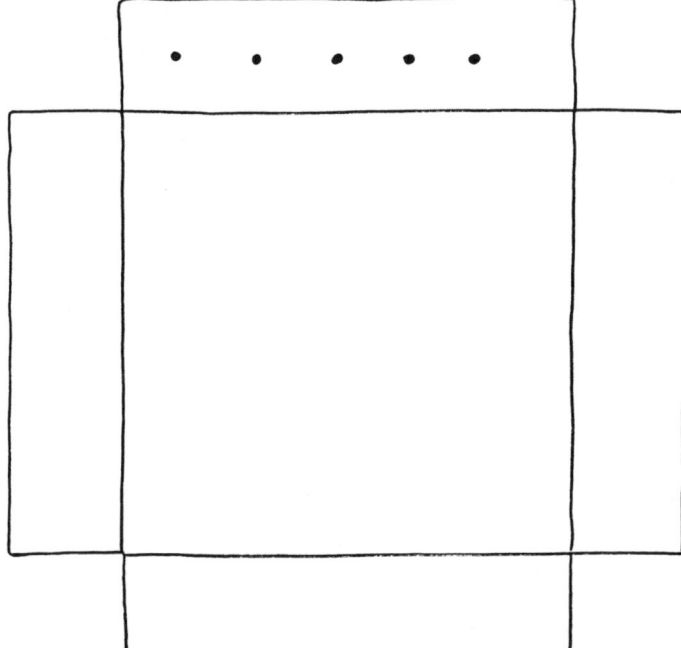

**Figure 85**

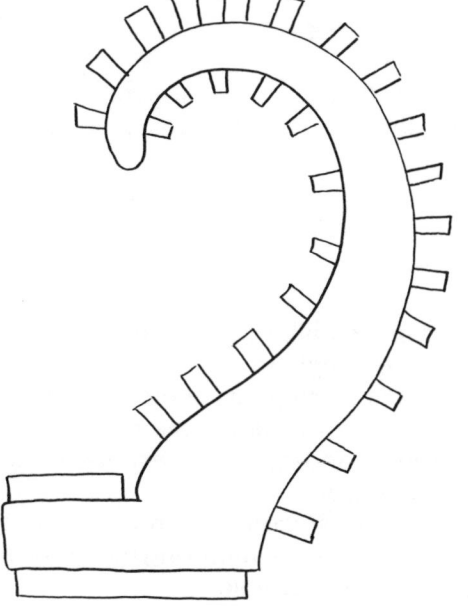

Fold on tabs and glue tabs together.

**Figure 86**

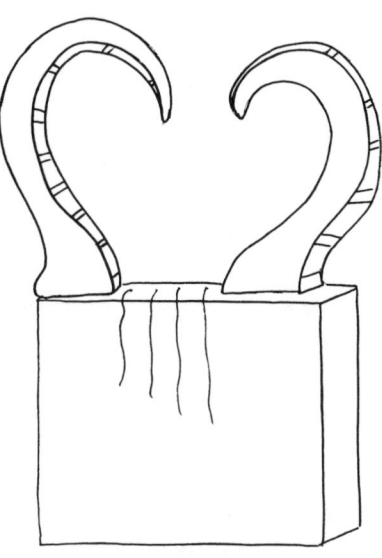

**Figure 88**

g. Cover the entire piece with papier mache and allow to dry completely. Caution children to keep strings free.
h. When mache is dry, the piece can be painted.
i. The dowel rod is glued to the top of the "kinnor" (Fig. 89), and strings are secured by tying.

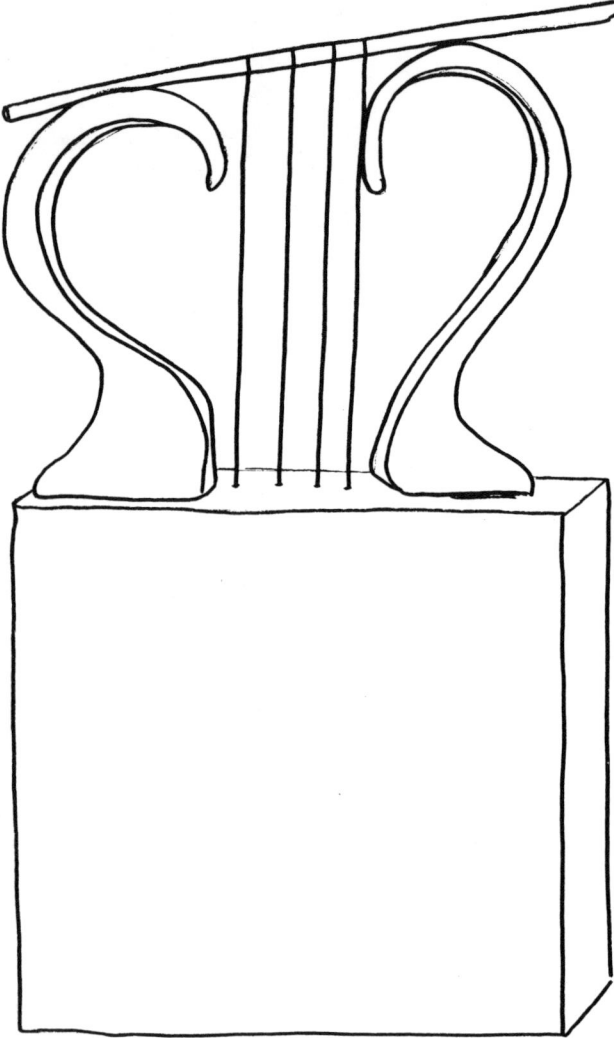

**Figure 89**

**Materials Needed:** K—3 patterns, glue, crayons, scissors, straws, string.

**How to Do It:**
a. Duplicate and distribute patterns shown in Figures 85 and 86 (two of 85, four of 86) and allow children to color.
b. Children cut and glue together.
c. Use a straw instead of the dowel rod and string or thread instead of guitar string.

# SOLOMON

*And, behold, I purpose to build an house unto the name of the Lord my God, as the Lord spake unto David my father, saying, the son, whom I will set upon thy throne in thy room, he shall build an house unto my name.*

1 Kings 5:5 KJV

### 60. Church Collage K—4

**Materials Needed:** cardboard, scissors, glue, magazines, and old greeting cards, yarn and tape.

**How to Do It:**
a. Pictures of various types of churches are cut out of magazines and other sources.
b. Pictures are glued to the cardboard in collage fashion.
c. An appropriate Bible verse such as Exodus 25:8 or "Remember the Sabbath Day to keep it holy" can be added to the collage.
d. Yarn is taped to the back to form a hanger.

### 61. Solomon's Temple 4—8

**Materials Needed:** cardboard, material scraps, rickrack, scissors or single-edge razor blades, glue.

**How to Do It:**
a. Read and discuss the Biblical description of the building of the temple in 2 Chronicles, chapters 2—4.
b. Divide your class into smaller groups, and assign a particular part of the temple to each.
c. Let each group make preliminary sketches of how they think their section of the temple might have looked. Walk around and give suggestions as to materials they might use.
d. Using cardboard, boxes and odds 'n' ends, students should build a temple model—following the Biblical descriptions as much as possible.

## FIERY FURNACE

*And he commanded the most mighty men that were in his army to bind Shadrach, Meshach and Abednego, and to cast them into the burning fiery furnace.*
            Daniel 3:20 KJV

### 62. Puppet Box  K—4

**Materials Needed:** shoe boxes (no lids), construction paper, cardboard, crayons or paints, scissors, glue.

**How to Do It:**

a. Outside of shoe boxes may be painted or covered with construction paper.
b. Shoe boxes are held so open end faces OUT. (See Fig. 90.)

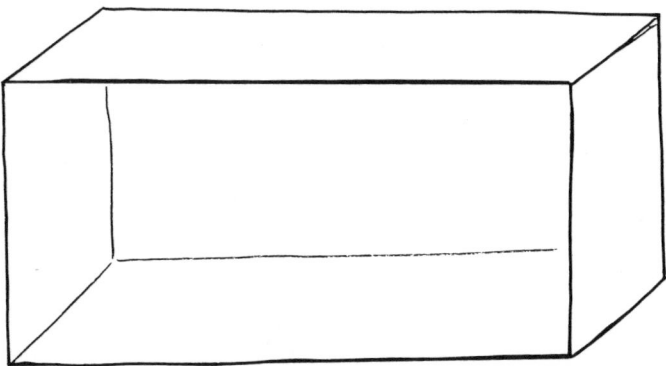

**Figure 90**

c. Help students make slits in bottom of shoe boxes as shown in Figure 91.

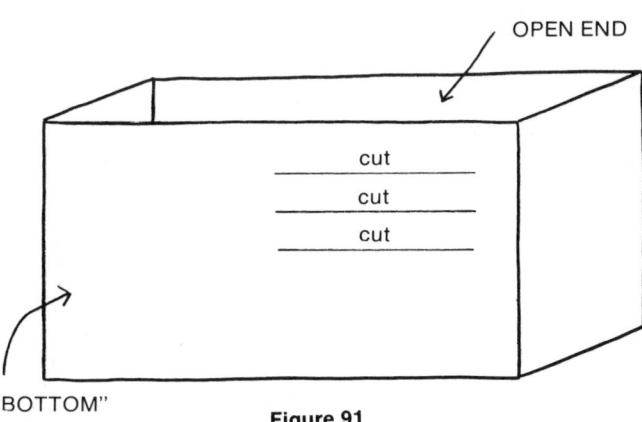

**Figure 91**

d. Students draw figures of King Nebuchadnezzar, Shadrach, Meshach, Abednego, Angel, and fire (or you may wish to duplicate Figures 92 through 97 which students can color and cut out. It is always best, however to encourage individual creativity rather than duplication.)

KING NEBUCHADNEZZAR

Children should decorate robe as desired.

**Figure 92**

SHADRACH　　　　　　　　　　　　　　　　　　　　MESHACH

**Figure 93**　　　　　　　　　　　　　　　　　　　**Figure 94**

**Figure 95**

**Figure 96**

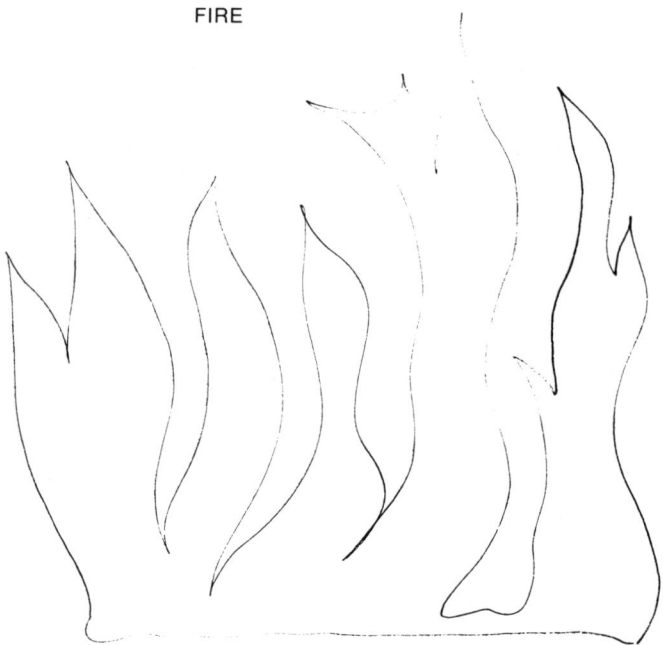

FIRE

**Figure 97**

e. Students should decorate inside of boxes to look like a dungeon and furnace. (See Fig. 98.)

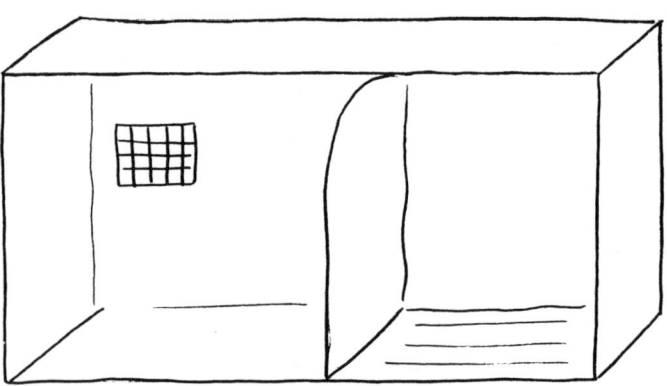

**Figure 98**

f. Glue figure of Nebuchadnezzar to section outside of the "furnace" area.
g. Glue strips of cardboard to all other figures.
h. Slip the "fire" through the front slit, Shadrach, Meshach, and Abednego through the second, and the angel figure through the third. Children can now use their puppet theatres to tell the story at home.

## 63. Idol Collage 4—8

**Materials Needed:** cardboard, magazines, glue, scissors.

**How to Do It:**
a. After discussing the story, encourage the students to name modern idols which people may put before the Lord.
b. Students find pictures of modern "idols" in magazines, cut them out, and paste in collage form on cardboard. A 3-D effect can be achieved by backing several pictures with small wads of cotton.
c. The collage may be completed by printing the First Commandment using paints or markers—or construction paper letters.
d. Yarn can be taped to the back of the finished picture to form a hanger.

## DANIEL

*Then the king commanded, and they brought Daniel, and cast him into the den of lions.*
*Daniel 6:16 KJV*

## 64. Stand-Up Lions K—3

**Materials Needed:** lightweight cardboard, yarn, construction paper, scissors and glue.

**How to Do It:**
a. Instruct students to fold a piece of cardboard in half.
b. The BODY (no head) of a lion is drawn on one side of the folded cardboard. (See Fig. 99.)

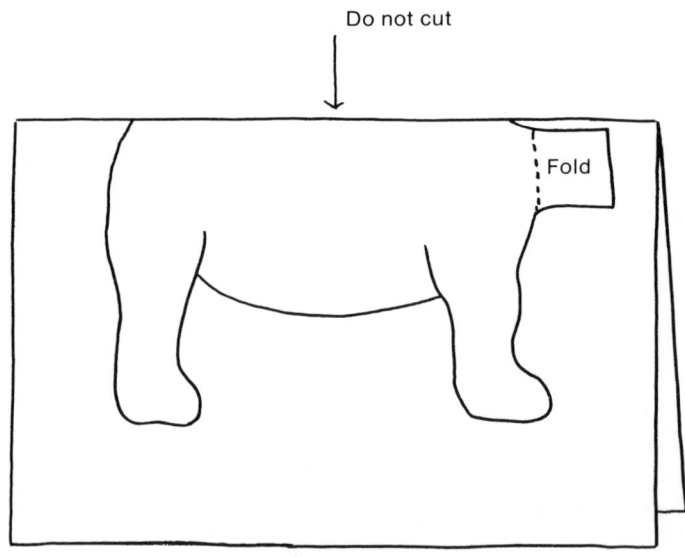

**Figure 99**

c. Pattern is cut out and glued at tabs.
d. A head is drawn as in Figure 100 and cut out. Construction paper eyes, nose, and whiskers can be added.

Features are added by cutting eyes, nose, whiskers, and mane from construction paper.

**Figure 100**

e. Glue head to the front of the body.
f. Add yarn for the mane and the tail.

**Variation:** *4—8* Older students will enjoy making murals or dioramas in connection with this story.

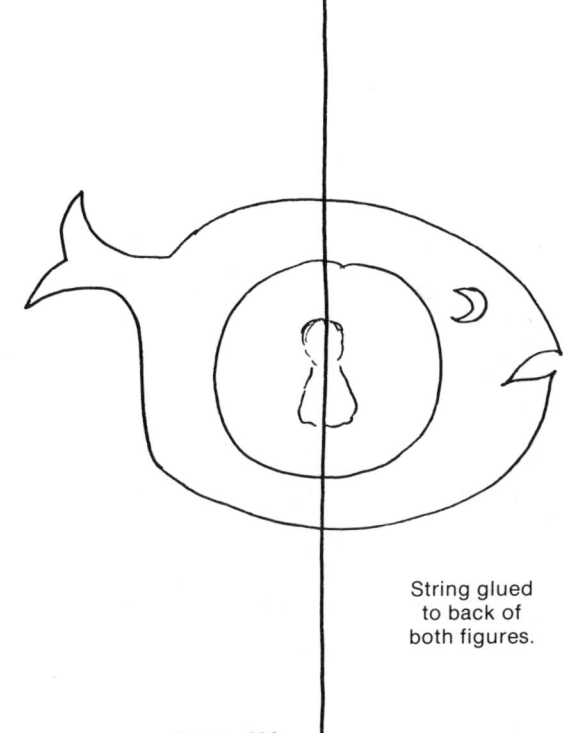

## JONAH

*Now the Lord had prepared a great fish to swallow up Jonah. And Jonah was in the belly of the fish three days and three nights.*

Jonah 1:17 KJV

### 65. Great Fish Mobile *K—8*

**Materials Needed:** construction paper, scissors, string, tape, and glue.

**How to Do It:**
a. Students should draw a large "open" fish and a figure of Jonah (or duplicate patterns in Fig. 101).
b. Students should cut out TWO of each.
c. String is glued to the fish and Jonah as shown in Figure 102.
d. Other patterns are then glued to the back—forming a "sandwich" with the string in the middle. This will allow the mobile to be viewed from both sides.

### 66. See-Through Fish *4—8*

**Materials Needed:** cardboard tubing (paper towel size), scissors, constructon paper, papier mache, glue.

**How to Do It:**
a. Students should cut a hole—about 1½" in width and 2—3" in length in the front top half of the cardboard tube. (See Fig. 103.)

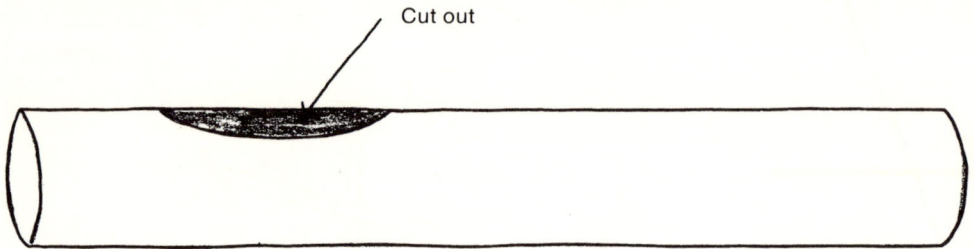

**Figure 103**

b. Using construction paper, pipe cleaners, clay, or other material, students should make a figure of Jonah and secure it to the bottom of the inside of the tube—just below the hole.
c. Using newspaper and papier mache mix, students then build up a fish figure. A hole should be left at the mouth and a slight "blow hole" left at the top (as shown in Fig. 104).

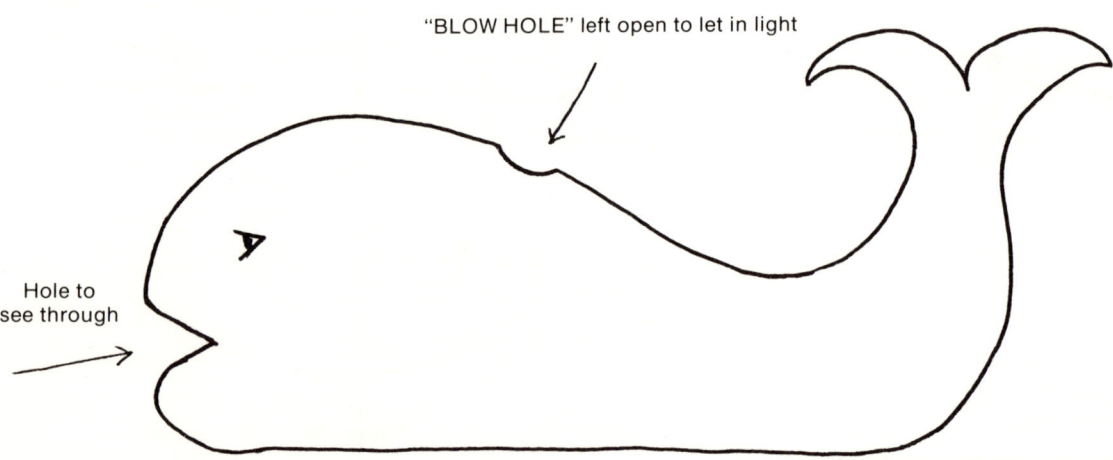

**Figure 104**

d. Students may paint the completed figure.

# Chapter 4: The New Testament

## CHRIST'S MINISTRY

*And He saith unto them, Follow Me, and I will make you fishers of men.*

Matthew 4:19 KJV

### 67. Fishers of Men Plaque K—4

**Materials Needed:** cardboard, hair nets or onion bags, crayons or paints, glue, construction paper.

**How to Do It:**
a. Children make a boat with mast as shown in Fig. 105.

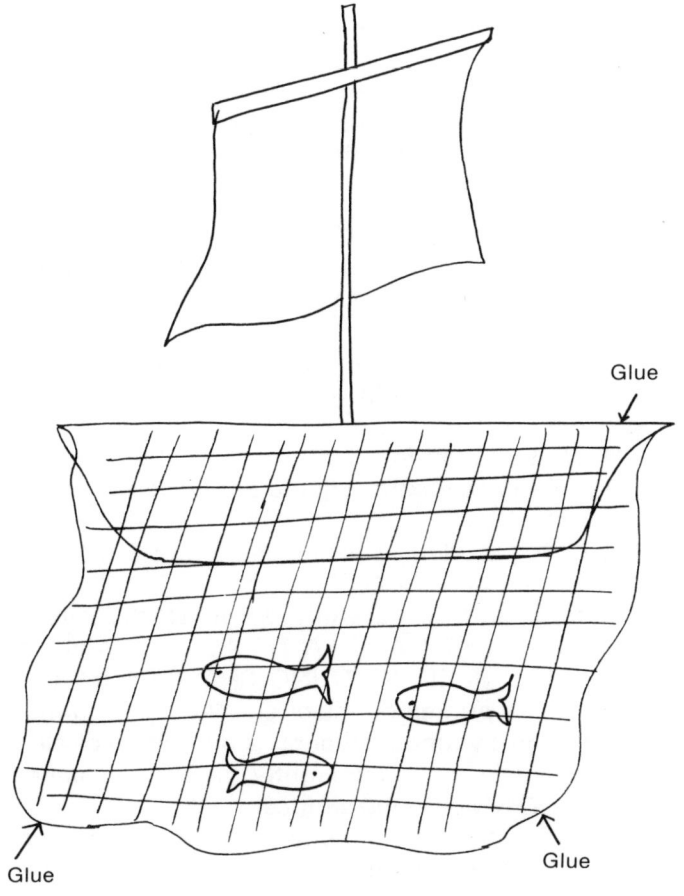

Figure 106

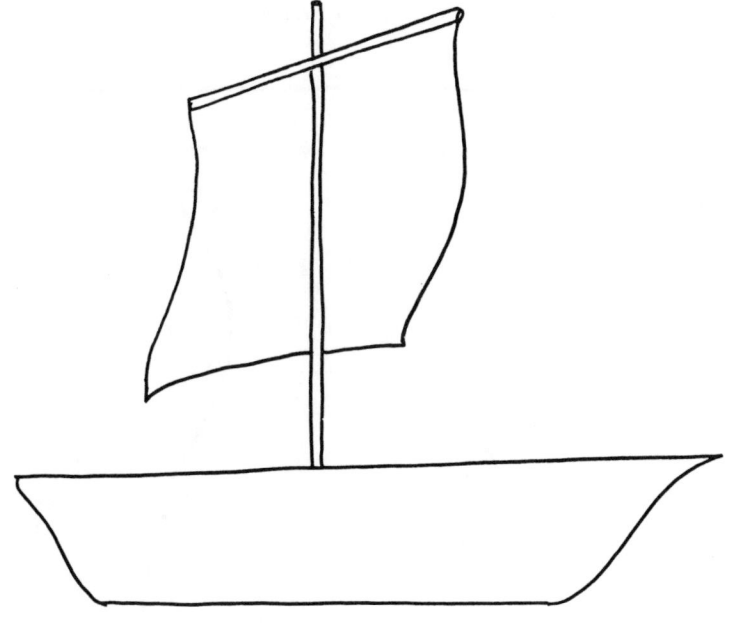

Figure 105

b. Boat parts are painted, cut out, and glued to cardboard background.
c. Several fish are cut from colored construction paper and glued to the background below the boat.
d. The onion bag or hair net is glued to the top edge of the boat and secured over the fish. (See Fig. 106.)
e. Students may write the words, "I will make you fishers of men," above the picture.
f. Yarn is attached to the back of the plaque for hanging.

### 68. Mobile 4—8

**Materials Needed:** clay, string, dowel rods or heavy wire, walnut shells, write drawing paper, toothpicks.

**How to Do It:**
a. Each student receives five or six walnut halves.
b. Each shell is filled with modeling clay.
c. A toothpick is inserted into the clay in each of the shells.
d. Masts are attached to the toothpicks.
e. Boats are hung with string. Students should exper-

iment with boat positions to balance mobiles properly.

*If ye have faith as a grain of mustard seed, ye shall say unto this mountain, Remove hence to yonder place; and it shall remove; and nothing shall be impossible unto you.*

*Matthew 17:20 KJV*

## 69. Paperweight K—8

**Materials Needed:** mustard seeds, small plastic butter dishes, vaseline, liquid plastic and catalyst (from any craft store), felt scraps, scissors, glue.

**How to Do It:**
a. Students cover the INSIDE of the butter dishes with a thin layer of vaseline (or, if your budget permits, you may wish to obtain a can of mold release spray from the craft store).
b. Mix plastic and catalyst according to directions. (You will have to help younger students with this process.)
c. Plastic is poured into butter dishes until they are HALF FILLED. Mixture should be allowed to gel for a few minutes.
d. Give each student a paper circle and a mustard seed.
e. Mustard seed is carefully glued to the circle. Words—"IF YE HAVE FAITH AS A GRAIN OF MUSTARD SEED, NOTHING SHALL BE IMPOSSIBLE" are printed on the circle. (Again—you may have to give younger students a preprinted circle.)
f. When plastic has gelled slightly, the circle is placed FACE DOWN onto the surface.
g. More mixed plastic is added until it reaches just below the rim of the dish.
h. Allow to harden completely.
i. Cups are removed and a piece of felt is glued to the bottom of the paperweight. Rough edges can be smoothed with a sheet of fine sandpaper.

## THE TEMPTATION OF CHRIST

*Then was Jesus led up of the spirit into the wilderness to be tempted of the devil.*

*Matthew 4:1 KJV*

## 70. Lead Us Not into Temptation Booklets K—8

**Materials Needed:** construction paper or heavy drawing paper, crayons or other coloring medium, hole puncher, yarn.

**How to Do It:**
a. Discuss the types of temptations which your students may encounter.
b. Students draw pictures illustrating these various temptations.
c. Encourage students to make up prayers dealing with their personal temptations.

**Variation:** *K—3* Younger students may find it difficult to draw pictures. Encourage them to use figures cut from books or magazines. They may also be given preprinted prayers.

## MARRIAGE AT CANA

*When the ruler of the feast had tasted the water that was made wine and knew not whence it was . . .*

*John 2:9 KJV*

## 71. Mosaic K—8

**Materials Needed:** construction paper, glue.

**How to Do It:**
a. Students first draw an outline of a water jug (Fig. 107) onto a large sheet of construction paper.

JAR

**Figure 107**

b. Students then TEAR small pieces of construction paper and glue them inside the "jar" in mosaic fashion (Fig. 108).

**Figure 108**

## 72. Moving Picture K—3

**Materials Needed:** construction paper, scissors, glue.

**How to Do It:**
a. Students are given copies of Figures 109 and 110.
b. The inside of the jar is cut out.

**Figure 109**

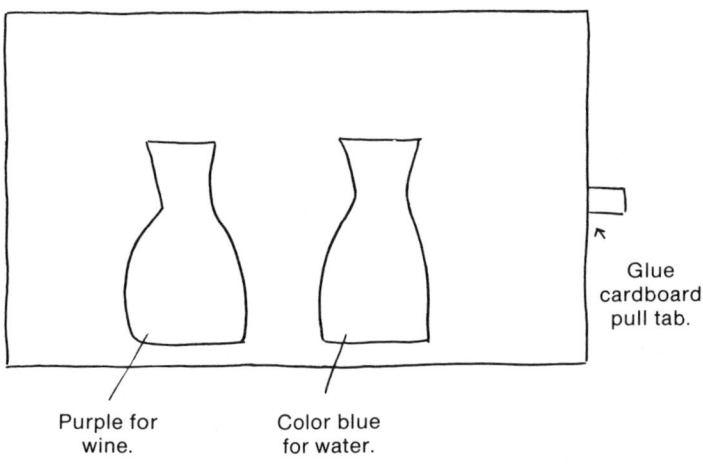

**Figure 110**

c. Picture is colored and glued BY EDGES ONLY to a background sheet of construction paper.
d. Figure 110 is inserted between the two sheets.

## LORD'S PRAYER

*And it came to pass, that, as He was praying in a certain place, when He ceased, one of His disciples said unto Him, Lord, teach us to pray.*

*Luke 11:1 KJV*

## 73. Sand Casting K—8

**Materials Needed:** sand, boxes or other deep containers, plaster.

**How to Do It:**
a. Place damp sand into the various containers.
b. Students make impression in the sand with ONE hand in a "praying hands" position. See Fig. 111.

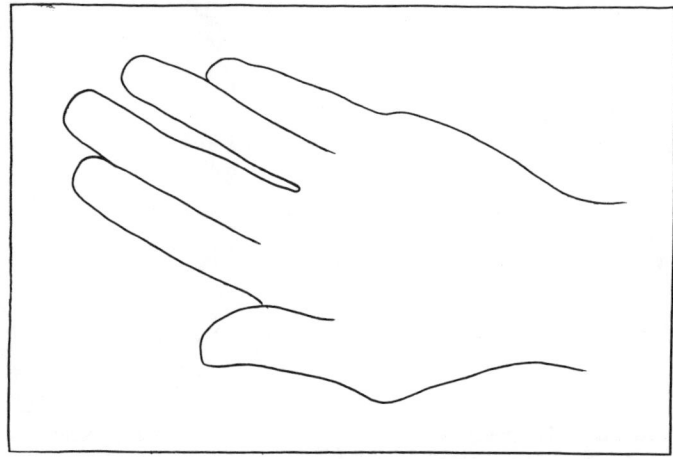

Hand is placed in sand PALM UP!    **Figure 111**

c. Mix plaster according to package directions.
d. Plaster is poured into the hand impression—filling in all cracks. Continue pouring plaster until there is a layer ½" in thickness.
e. Before plaster sets completely, a wire hanger should be inserted at the top.
f. When plaster has set completely, it can be removed from the form. Excess sand can be brushed off with a paint brush.

**Variation:** 5—8
**Materials Needed:** gallon or half-gallon milk containers (or grocery boxes lined with plastic bags), sand, plaster, wood scraps.

**How to Do It:**
a. Fill containers with *damp* sand.
b. Students hold both hands in a "praying hands" position and insert into the sand fingers first—as if "diving." (For this project, students can fold hands for equally dramatic results.) Hands should be inserted as far as the wrists.
c. Before pouring plaster, students should make sure that the impression of their hands comes out clearly.
d. Plaster is mixed to creamy consistency and poured SLOWLY into the sand mold.
e. When plaster has dried *completely,* hands sculpture is removed.
f. Sculpture is cleaned and attached to a piece of sanded scrap wood using a heavy glue.
g. To finish off—and to secure firmly—the base of the sculpture is surrounded with hardening plaster around the wrists.

## LOVE

*Thou shalt love the Lord thy God with all thy heart, and with all thy soul, and with all thy mind ... And ... thou shalt love thy neighbor as thyself.*

Matthew 22:36-40

### 74. Quilling Project K—8

**Materials Needed:** white drawing paper or quilling paper, toothpicks, glue, cardboard.

**How to Do It:**
a. Students make two basic quilling figures as shown in Fig. 112.

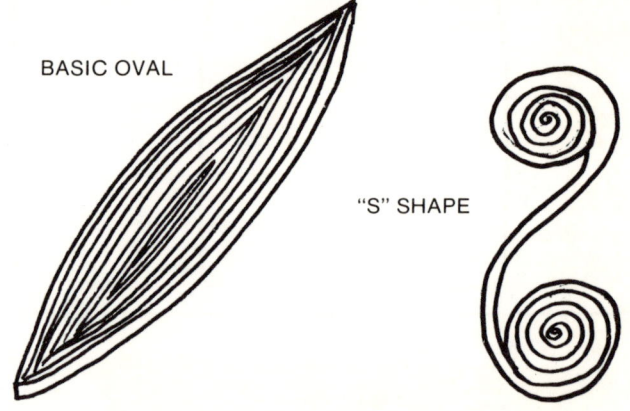

**Wind quilling paper around the tip of a toothpick. Pinch both ends to form the oval shape.

For the "S" shape, roll each end of the quilling paper into a coil—leaving a connecting strip as shown.

**Figure 112**

b. The word LOVE is formed using the basic oval (Fig. 113).

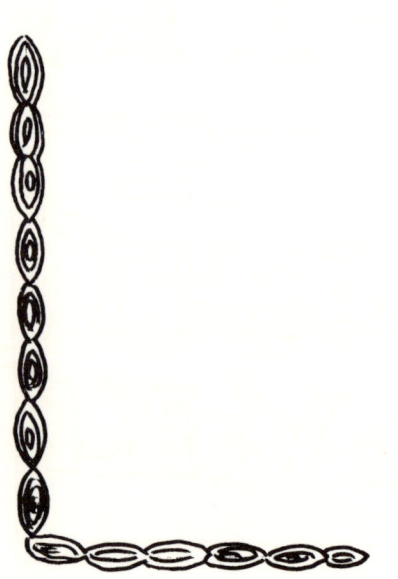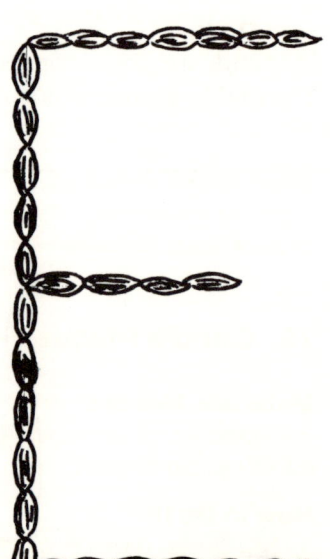

**Figure 113**

64

c. The "S" form is used as a decorative edge (Fig. 114).

Figure 114

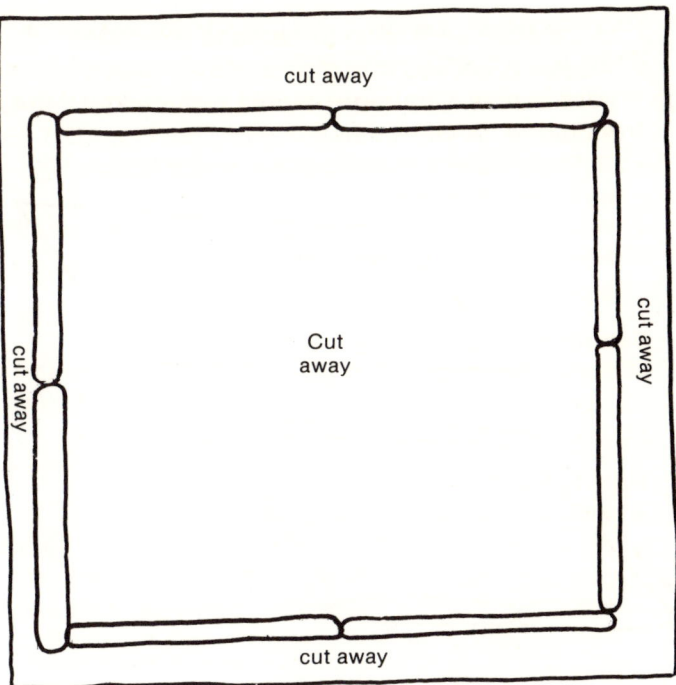

Figure 115

b. Cut out TWO sheets of wax paper—both the same size—slightly larger than the area inside the frame.
c. From cellophane, students cut out a cross and the words, "I AM THE LIGHT OF THE WORLD."
d. Words are placed on one sheet of wax paper.
e. When words and cross are in place, the second sheet of wax paper is CAREFULLY placed over the first, and the two are ironed together (Fig. 116).

Figure 116

d. Word is glued to cardboard covered with construction paper.

**Variation:** K—3
Students in this age group can get very good results using a pencil instead of a toothpick.

*Then spake Jesus again unto them, saying, I am the Light of the world; he that followeth Me shall not walk in darkness, but shall have the light of life.*
*John 8:12 KJV*

**75. Candle Plaque** 4—8

**Materials Needed:** craft sticks, wax paper, colored cellophane, glue, modeling clay, jar lids, iron, votive candles, cardboard.

**How to Do It:**
a. Students glue 8 craft sticks to a sheet of light cardboard and, after glue has dried, cut all excess cardboard away. (See Fig. 115.)

65

f. This wax paper "sandwich" is glued to the craft stick frame (on the cardboard side).

g. Students now glue eight more craft sticks to the front of the frame—completing it. (See Fig. 117.)

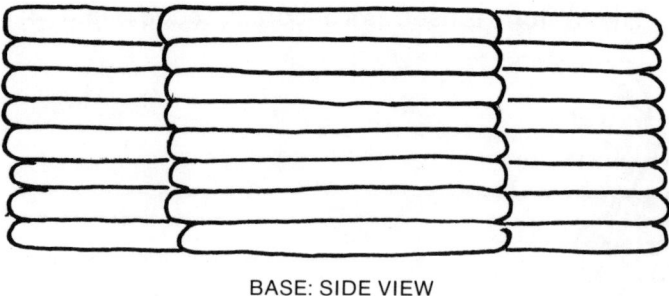

BASE: SIDE VIEW

BASE: TOP VIEW

**Figure 118**

Wax paper "sandwich" is glued to the craft stick base—on the cardboard side.

Picture is covered with a top layer of craft sticks.

Glue to front

**Figure 117**

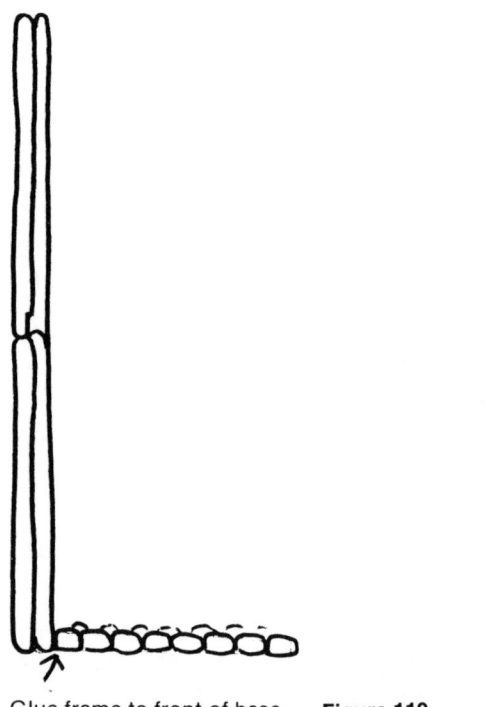

Glue frame to front of base   **Figure 119**

FRONT VIEW

SIDE VIEW

**Figure 120**

h. While the frame is drying, students make the stand as shown in Fig. 118.

i. After eight sets of craftsticks have been glued together, the frame is glued in an UPRIGHT POSITION. (Fig. 119.)

j. One set of four craft sticks is added to the front for support as in Figure 120.

k. Fill jar lid with clay and glue to the back of the platform. (See Fig. 121.)

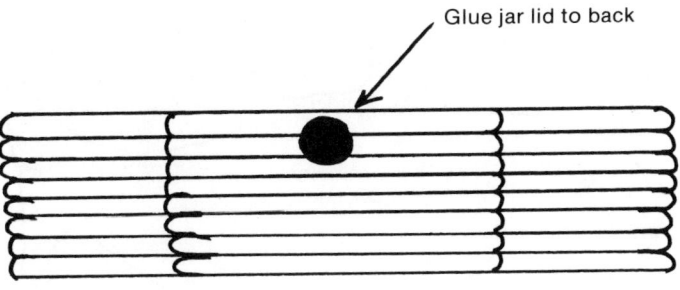

**Figure 121**

l. Place candles in the clay. Light will show through wax paper and cellophane—creating a stained-glass effect.

**Variation:** K—3
a. Have children follow steps 1—7 above.
b. Glue on yarn or hanger.
c. "Stained glass" picture can be hung from a window.

*And Jesus went about all Galilee, teaching in their synagogues, and preaching the gospel of the kingdom, and healing all manner of sickness and all manner of disease among the people.*

*Matthew 4:23 KJV*

### 76. Without Words K—3 Variation: 4—8

**Materials Needed:** black and white construction paper, glue, scissors.

**How to Do It:**
a. After discussing the miracles of Christ, ask your students to think of a way they could tell about a mriacle WITHOUT USING ANY WORDS.
b. Let students choose a miracle they would like to illustrate.
c. A silhouette is cut from black construction paper and glued to a white background. (Geometric figures should be cut out and glued together to form figures.)

**Figure 122**

d. Children might enjoy guessing the miracles their classmates illustrate.

**Variation:** *4—8*

Older children might enjoy using india ink—experimenting with pen and ink or brush and ink.

## DISCIPLES AND APOSTLES

### 77. Ichthys Mobile *K—8*

**Materials Needed:** string, heavy-duty cardboard, hole puncher, tape.

**How to Do It:**
a. Students draw a large fish and five smaller fish (Fig. 123).

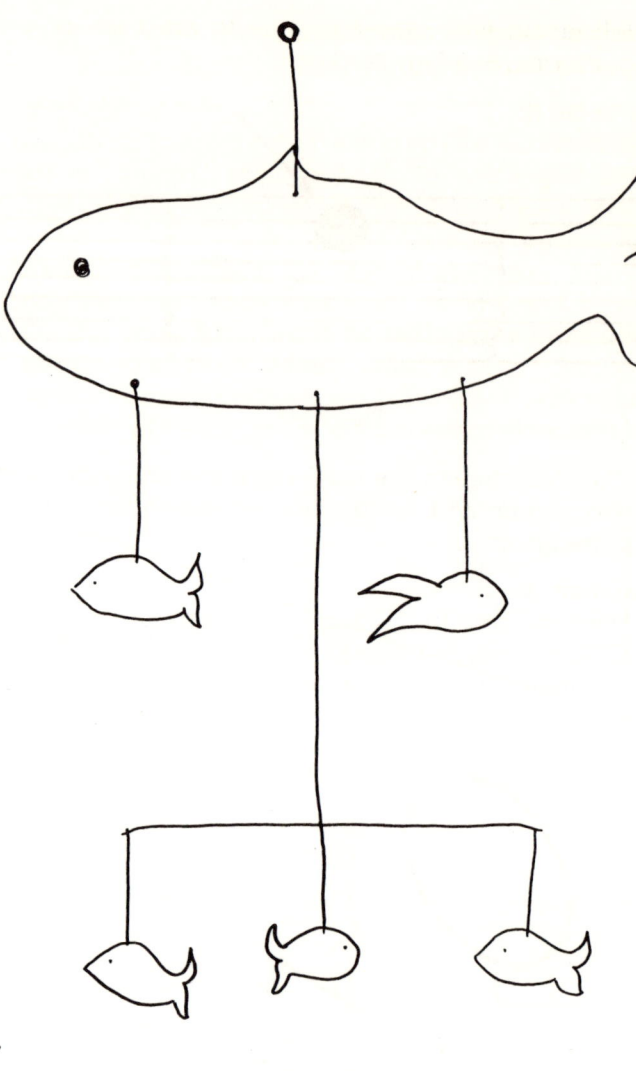

**Figure 124**

**Variations:** *5—8*
a. If jigsaw is available, let students make fish from balsa wood.
b. Fish can be formed from flexible wire.

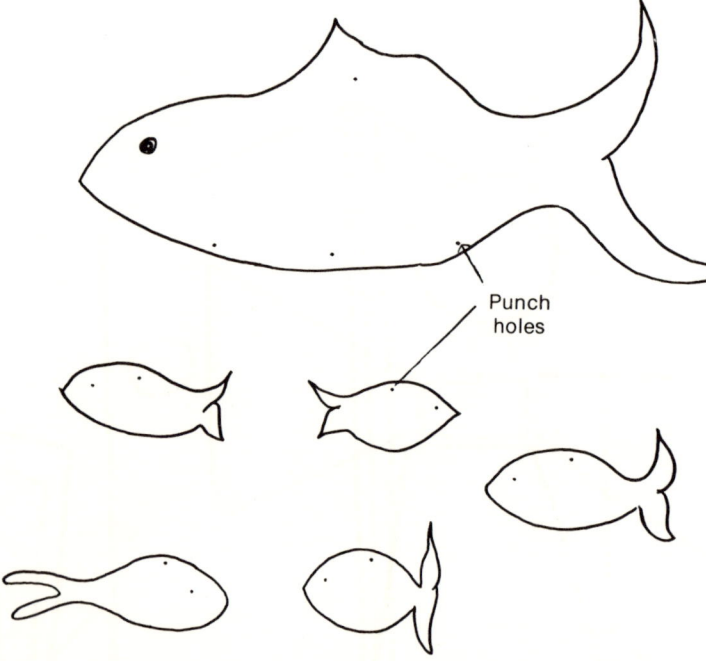

**Figure 123**

b. A hole is punched at the top of the larger fish, and three holes at the bottom.
c. A hole is punched at the top of each of the smaller fish.
d. Attach as shown in Figure 124.

*Grant unto us that we may sit, one on Thy right hand and the other on Thy left hand, in Thy glory.*
*Mark 10:37 KJV*

### 78. Hall of Fame *3—8*

James and John, the sons of Zebedee, voiced a normal human desire—to be recognized and given honor and, perhaps, some power. What if there were an Apostle's Hall of Fame? Who would be honored? What type of display would that person have?

**Materials Needed:** cardboard, paint, odds 'n' ends, glue, scissors, heavy-duty tape.

**How to Do It:**
a. Students cut a large circle from a piece of cardboard (the larger the circle, the more "rooms" in the piece.) A circle 12" in diameter makes four fairly nice-sized "rooms."
b. "Walls" are made from 6" x 8" pieces of cardboard taped together on the inside edge—forming right angles to each other as shown in Figure 125. (Of course, if base is larger, "walls" must be of comparable size. A wall must always reach from the center of the circle to the outside edge. (See Fig. 126.)

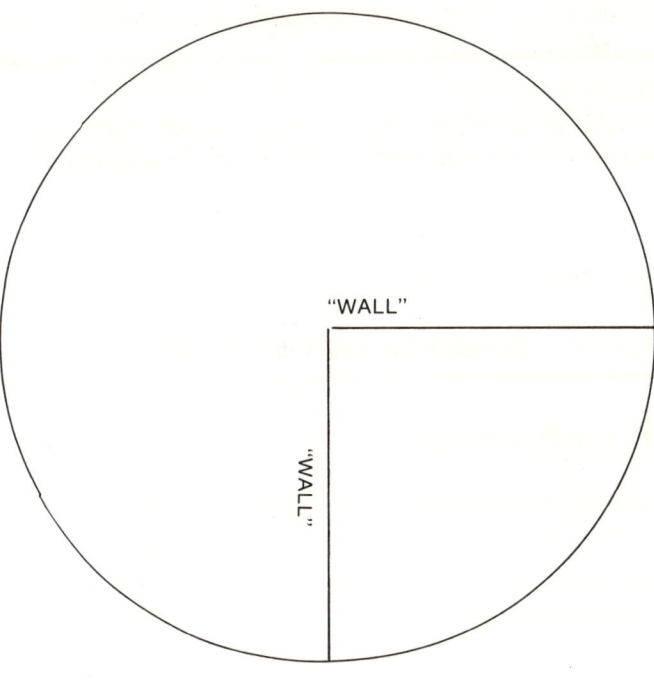

"HALL OF FAME: TOP VIEW"

**Figure 126**

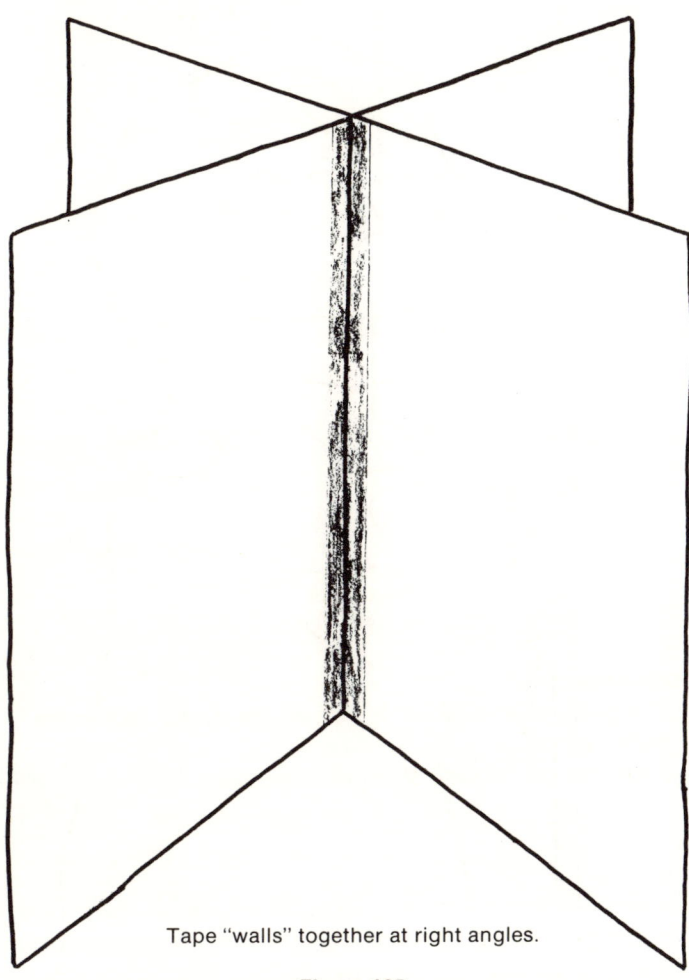

Tape "walls" together at right angles.

**Figure 125**

c. "Rooms" are attached to the base with heavy-duty tape. (See Fig. 127.)
d. Using paints and odds 'n' ends, students decorate the "rooms" to depict the important events in the disciples' lives.

**Variation:** K—2
Younger children can make this a group project and be quite successful with it.

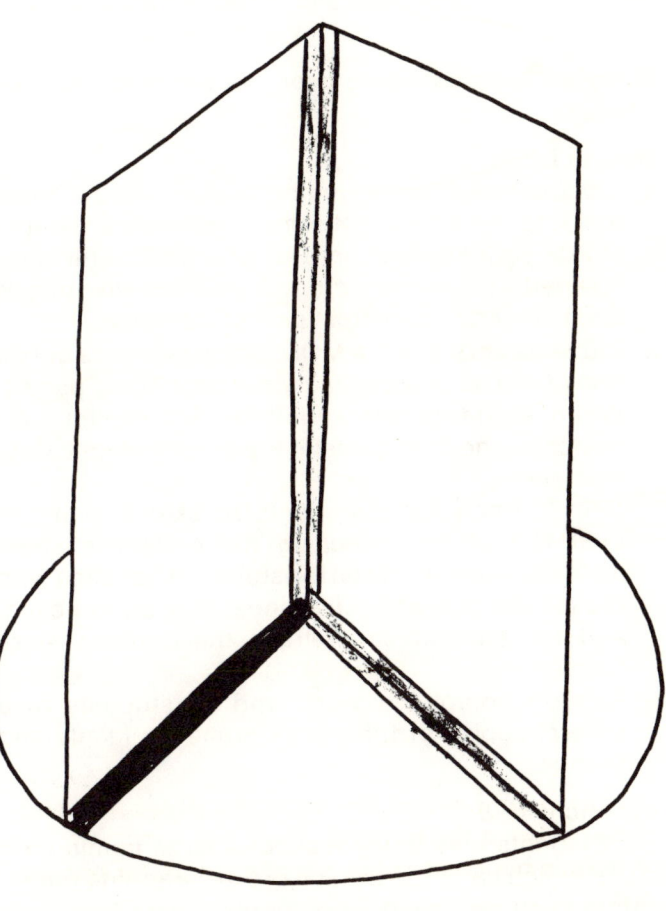

**Figure 127**

# PARABLES

*And a certain Samaritan, as he journeyed, came where he was: and when he saw him, he had compassion on him.*

Luke 10:33 KJV

## 79. Samaritan Scrapbook K—4

**Materials Needed:** paper, scissors, glue, magazines and catalogs.

**How to Do It:**
a. Discuss how children in this age group can be "Good Samaritans" (help at home, helping a younger child, etc.).
b. Using pictures cut from magazines and catalogs, children illustrate several ways they can be "Good Samaritans."

## 80. Good Samaritan—Year 4—8

Here's a way to give your older students an opportunity to apply this story to their own world and lives.

**Materials Needed:** scrap paper, duplicating masters, pencils.

**How to Do It:**
a. Discuss how this story might have been told if Christ told it today. (You'll get some interesting answers.)
b. Divide your students into smaller groups (illustrators, letterers, writers, etc.). Or you may wish to give each student a particular part of the story.
c. Students illustrate the MODERN version in a comic book form, first sketching ideas onto scrap paper.
d. When students are satisfied with preliminary sketches, they can transfer them to the duplicating masters.*

*HINT: Encourage students to sketch pictures LIGHTLY at first—keeping the protective sheet inside the master. When the student is satisfied with the results, the protective sheet may be removed, and the student can retrace the drawing more firmly.

e. Run off completed work, and let students take several copies of their book home for family and friends.

**Variation:** 4—8
Students may enjoy making a large comic strip mural which can be drawn on brown wrapping paper, painted and displayed for other classes and adults to see.

*I am the Good Shepherd: The Good Shepherd giveth His life for the sheep.*

John 10:11 KJV

## 81. Good Shepherd Plaque K—8

**Materials Needed:** K—3 cardboard, cotton, duplicated patterns, scissors, glue.

**How to Do It:**
a. Duplicate and distribute patterns of sheep and shepherd (Figs. 128 and 129).

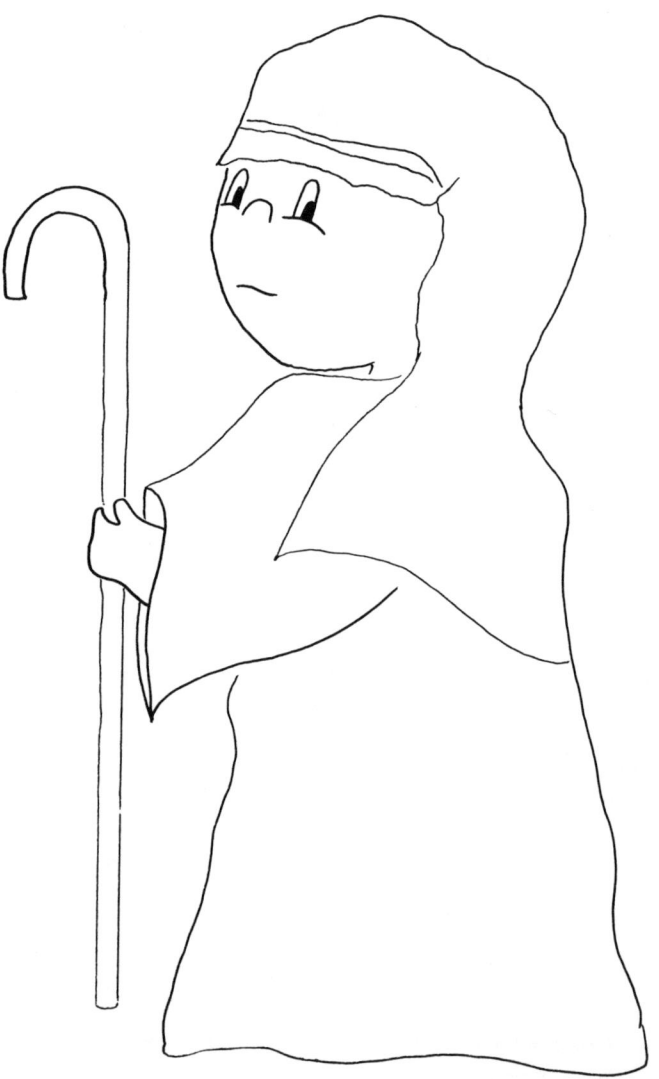

**Figure 128**

Glue cotton to sheep's body

**Figure 129**

b. Students cut out both figures and glue to cardboard background—which can be colored or painted first.
c. Cotton is glued to the sheep—except to the face.
d. Shepherd can be colored or—if your students are able—they may enjoy gluing fabric pieces to the figure for clothing.

**Materials Needed:** 4—8 cardboard, fabric, glue, liquid starch, scissors, cotton.

**How to Do It:**
a. Duplicate and distribute patterns shown in Figures 128 and 129 (or encourage students to draw their own figures).
b. Figures are cut out. Cotton is glued to the sheep, and fabric—dipped in liquid starch—is draped over the shepherd figure.
c. A background scene is drawn or painted onto a sheet of cardboard while figures are drying. Dried twigs and leaves add a special touch if glued to the scene.
d. Several layers of small cardboard strips are glued to the BACK of both figures.
e. Figures are glued to the background and will stand out.

*No man, when he hath lighted a candle, covereth it with a vessel or putteth it under a bed; but setteth it on a candlestick, that they which enter in may see the light.*
*Luke 8:16 KJV*

### 82. Banner K—8

**Materials Needed:** felt, dowel rods, glue, scissors.

**How to Do It:**
a. Banners may be as large as supplies, time, and student ability permit.
b. Older students may wish to sketch out their own banner to illustrate the words, "THY WORD IS A LAMP UNTO MY FEET." Remind students that banners are like posters—they tell a message simply.
c. For younger students, duplicate and distribute the basic pattern shown in Figure 130.

**Figure 130**

### 83. Candle Lamp 5—8

**Materials Needed:** self-hardening clay (or ceramic clay if a kiln is available), votive candles, soup cans, vaseline.

**How to Do It:**

a. Students develop a basic "lamp" shape around a soup can coated with vaseline (this will create a space for the candle). Clay should also be placed UNDER the can. All cracks and spaces should be carefully smoothed out to avoid cracking while drying or in the kiln.
b. When students are satisfied with the "lamps," the cans are carefully removed and projects allowed to dry.
c. Dried projects are painted, glazed, or covered with a layer of clear shellac.
d. Candle is placed in the finished ceramic piece.

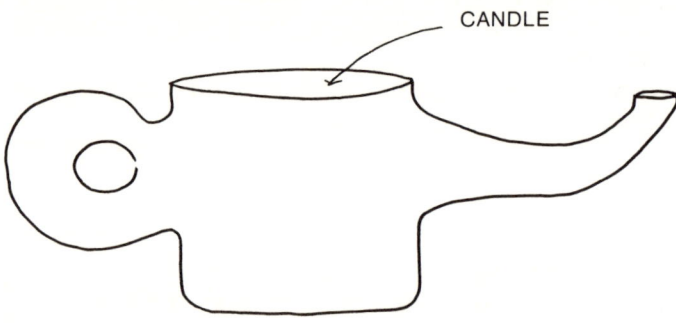

**Figure 131**

**Variation:** K—4

Younger students can make free-form candle holders.

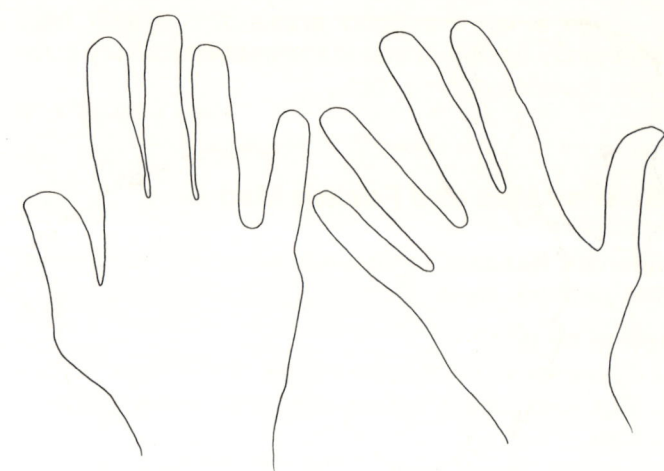

PALMS UP

**Figure 132**

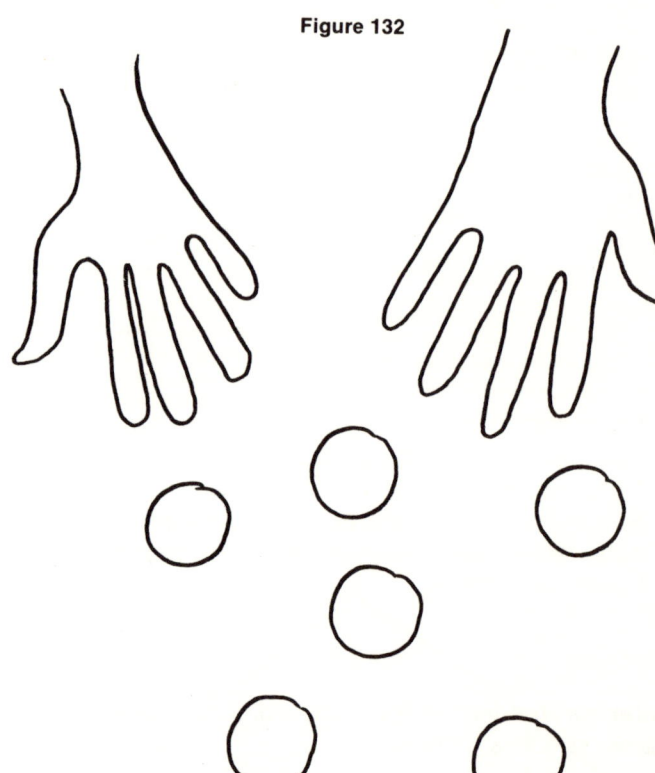

**Figure 133**

*For the kingdom of heaven is as a man traveling into a far country, who called his own servants, and delivered unto them his goods. And unto one he gave five talents, to another two, and to another one. . . .*

*Matthew 25:14-29*

**84. Talent Collage** 5—8

**Materials Needed:** cardboard, construction paper, scissors, glue.

**How to Do It:**

a. Students trace a partner's hands PALMS UP. (See Fig. 132.)
b. A 12" x 18" cardboard is painted or covered with fabric (or a collage of pictures illustrating various human traits and talents).
c. Students cut out and glue the tracings of their own hands onto the background.
d. Several cardboard circles representing "talents" are cut out and glued below the hands as shown in Figure 133.
e. On each circle, students may illustrate or write in the various talents God has given them (music, sense of humor, athletic ability, a way with animals, etc.). This is a great opportunity for students to share POSITIVE thoughts about one another.

**Variation:** 5—8

The saying, "What you are is God's gift to you. What you make of yourself is your gift to God!" lends itself well to such projects as collages, murals, and banners.

72

*. . . and when the flood arose, the stream beat vehemently upon that house and could not shake it: for it was founded upon a rock.*

*Luke 6:48-49 KJV*

## 85. Wise Man and Foolish Man K—3

**Materials Needed:** cardboard, scissors, magazines, glue, pebbles, sand.

**How to Do It:**
a. Duplicate and distribute copies of the "rock" house (Fig. 134), "sand" house (Fig. 135), and water (Fig. 136).

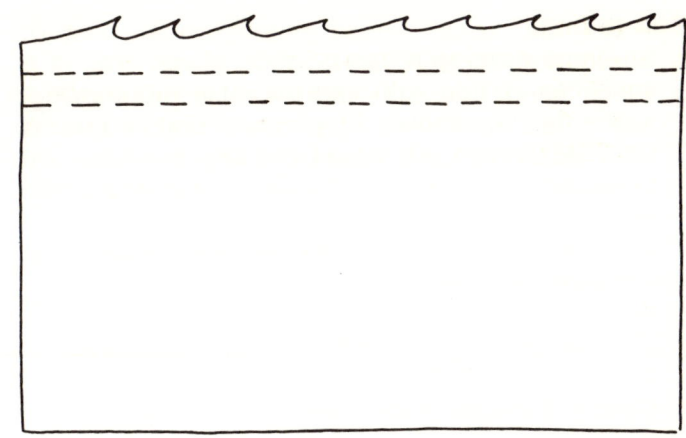

Top line is folded AWAY from student; Bottom line folded TOWARD the student.

**Figure 136**

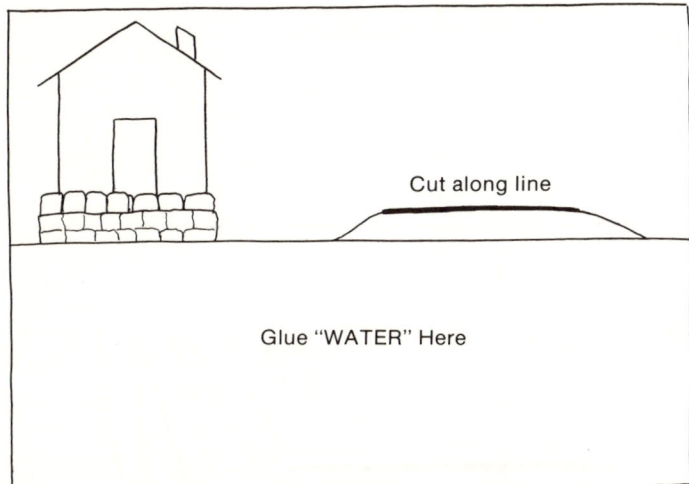

**Figure 134**

b. The children should color all pictures. Fish can be added to the water if children desire (fabric, construction paper, and various odds 'n' ends will add extra color).
c. Water and "sand" house are cut out.
d. The dark heavy line at the top edge of the sand is cut.
e. A long cardboard strip is taped or glued to the back of the "sand" house. (See Fig. 137.)

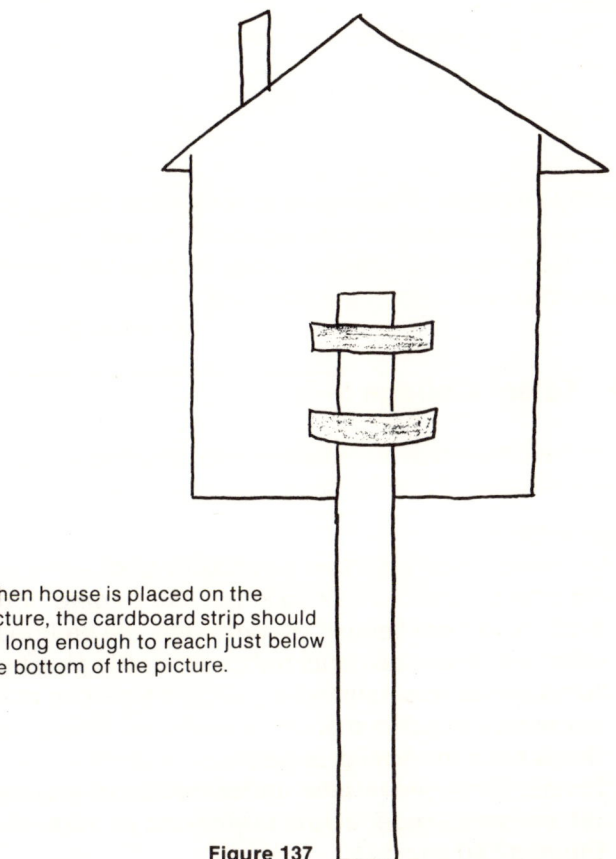

When house is placed on the picture, the cardboard strip should be long enough to reach just below the bottom of the picture.

**Figure 137**

Children color and cut out

**Figure 135**

73

f. Place the "rock" house picture on a sheet of cardboard. DO NOT GLUE.
g. Place "sand" house through the slit in the sand (Fig. 138). Pull cardboard strip down until house is covered by the sand. (See Fig. 139.)

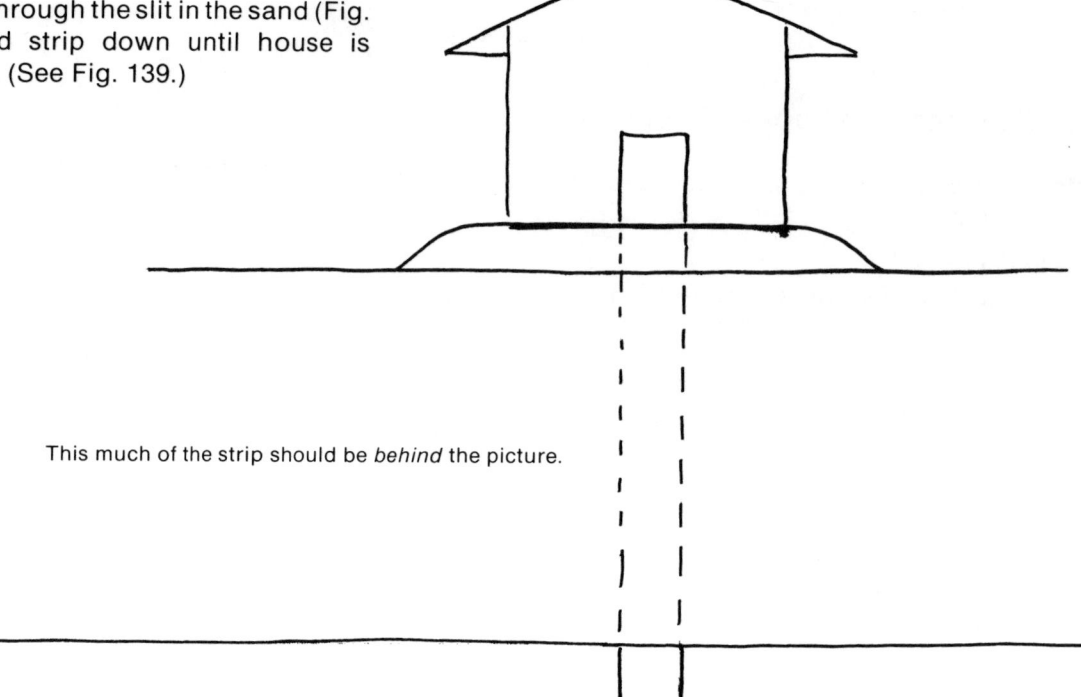

This much of the strip should be *behind* the picture.

**Figure 138**

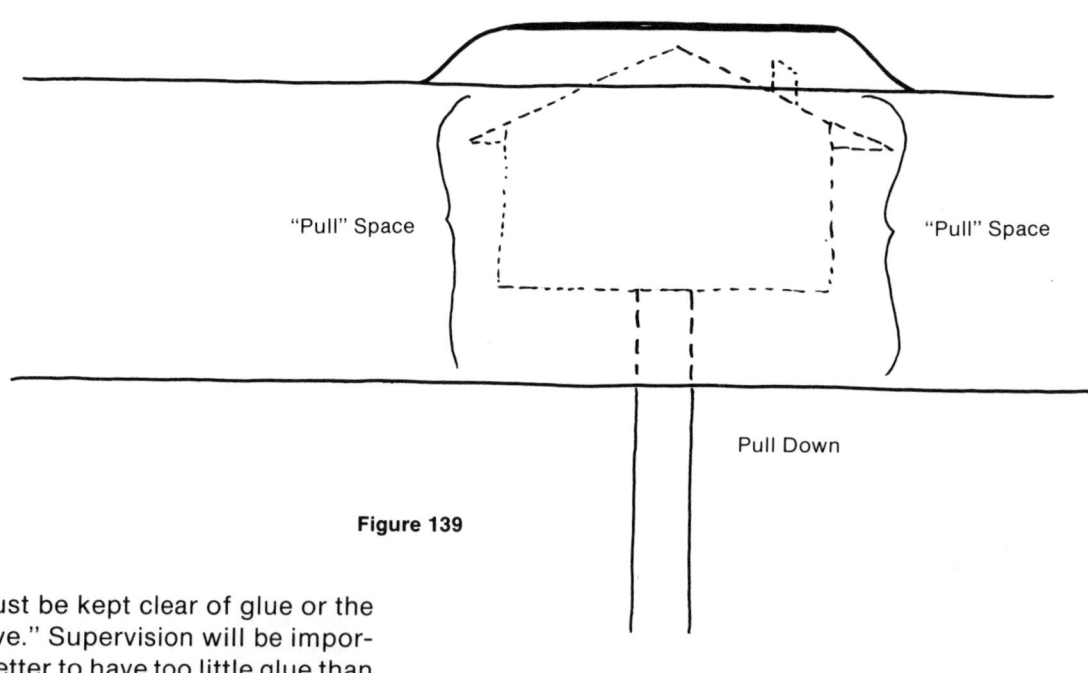

"Pull" Space   "Pull" Space

Pull Down

**Figure 139**

h. This "pull space" must be kept clear of glue or the picture will not "move." Supervision will be important here. It will be better to have too little glue than too much at this point. You—or parents—can make necessary adjustments.
i. Students may now glue pebbles under the "rock" house and sprinkle sand under the "sand" house.
j. Water is now glued to the completed picture. (See Figures 140 and 141.)

74

**Figure 140**

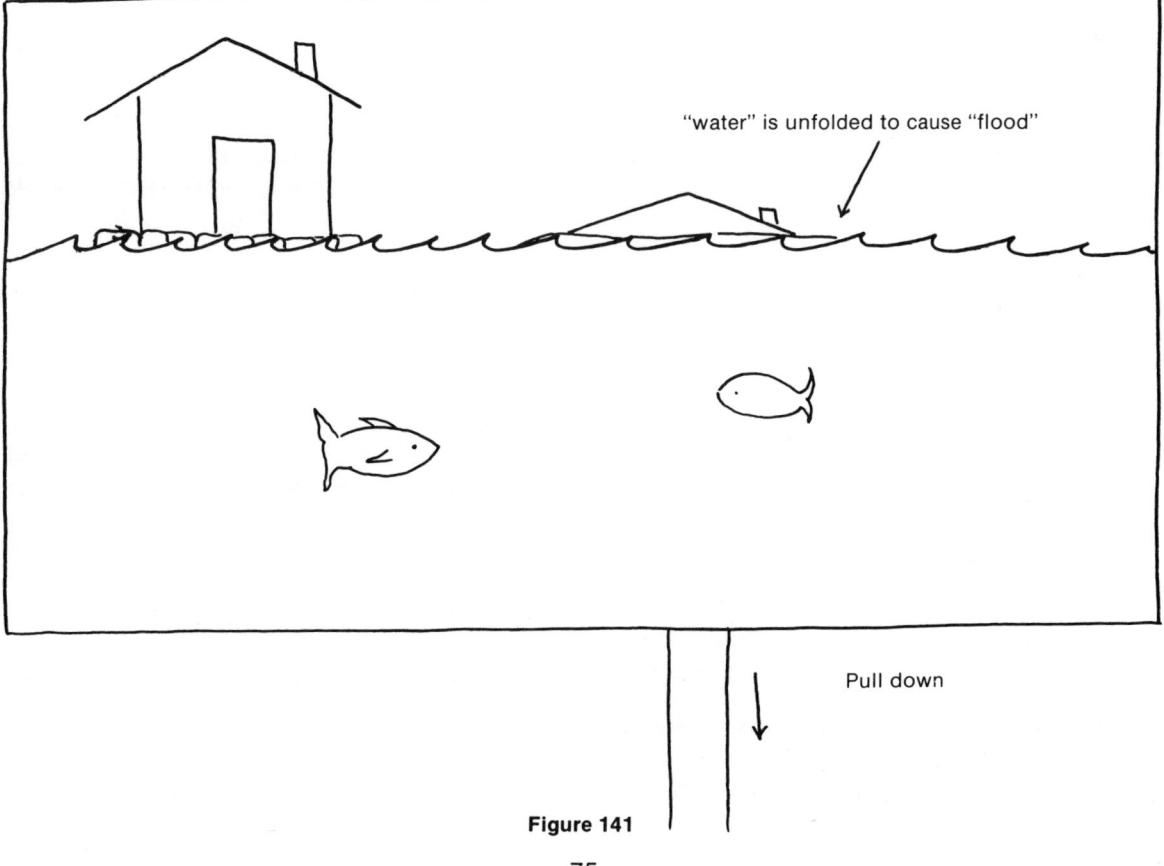

**Figure 141**

*Then shall the kingdom of heaven be likened unto ten virgins, which took their lamps, and went forth to meet the bridegroom. . . .*

*Matthew 25:1-13*

## 86. Lantern 4—8

**Materials Needed:** cardboard, colored cellophane, tape, scissors, black acrylics, brushes, black construction paper.

**How to Do It:**

a. Each student receives a sheet of cardboard 6" x 20".
b. Cardboard is folded width-ways in four equal sections—each section five inches wide. (See Fig. 142.)

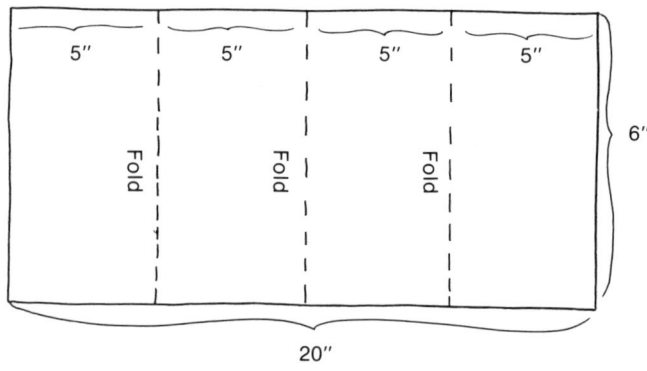

**Figure 142**

c. The center of each section is cut out—leaving a one inch border (Fig. 143).

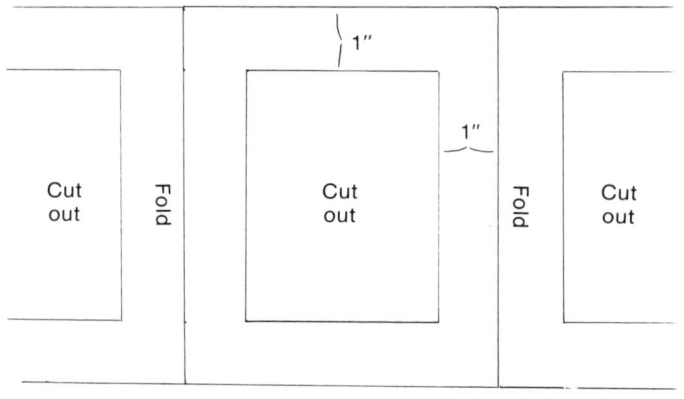

**Figure 143**

d. Silhouettes illustrating Bible stories are cut out and glued to the back of cellophane sheets. These sheets are taped to the back of the lantern.
e. The cardboard is folded on the creases—cellophane on the INSIDE.
f. The open end of the lantern is secured with black masking tape.
g. Students may paint frame with black acrylic paint.

**Variation:** 7—8
**Materials Needed:** cellophane, construction paper, heavy-duty tape, old lampshades (from home).

**How to Do It:**

a. Students cut out panels from the lampshade as shown in Figure 144.

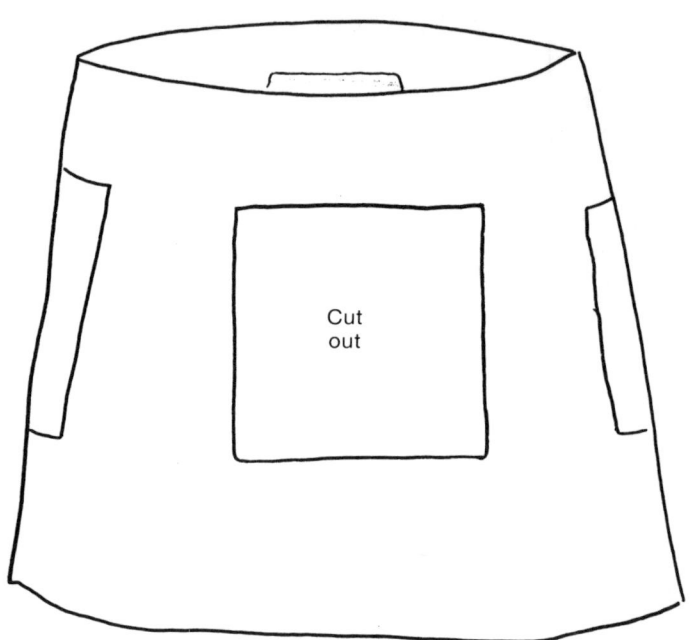

**Figure 144**

b. Silhouettes are cut from black construction paper, glued to cellophane and taped to the INSIDE of the lampshade.

*Either what woman having ten pieces of silver, if she lose one piece, doth not light a candle, and sweep the house, and seek diligently till she find it? . . .*

*Luke 15:8-10 KJV*

## 87. Lost Coin Picture K—3

**Materials Needed:** crayons, scissors, tape, duplicated patterns.

**How to Do It:**

a. Duplicate and distribute sheets as shown in Figures 145 and 146.

**Figure 145**

Cut out boxes and tape or glue behind flaps in LOST COIN picture

**Figure 146**

b. Children color and cut along three sides of each flap in Figure 145. Bible verses and coin picture are also cut out.

c. Bible verse and coin boxes are taped behind openings. (See Fig. 147.)

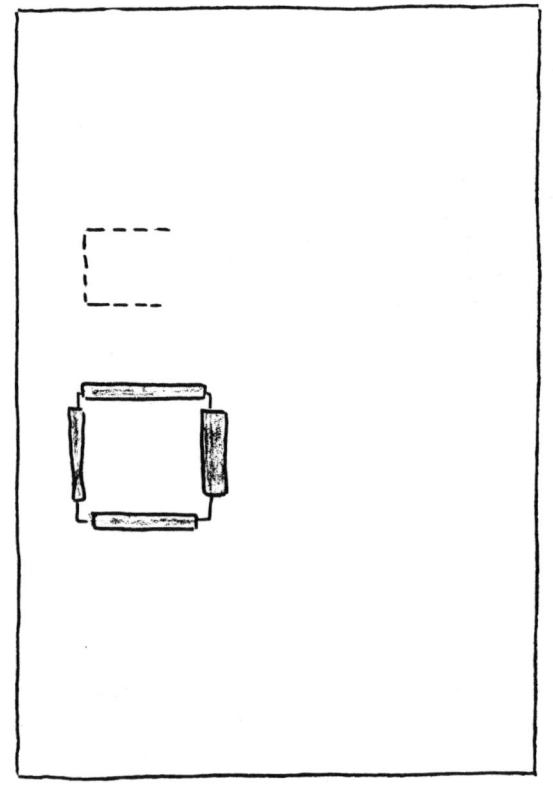

BACK

FRONT
(Coin may be placed anywhere children desire)

**Figure 147**

## Appendix I: Basic Materials

Most church-school groups panic when they hear the word "materials." Limited budgets very often make these groups resort to "color the picture" projects. Yet, the ingredients for a successful, diversified arts and crafts program can be found in the homes—and in the trash barrels—of your students.

If space is limited and these materials cannot be collected and stored, send a note home approximately two weeks before the project is scheduled—advising parents of your particular needs.

### General Materials
Newspaper—LOTS OF IT!
Cardboard—all sizes and weights; again, STOCK UP!
Scrap paper—you'll be surprised how much paper can be "recycled" in this manner.

### For Collages
Magazines and catalogs with LOTS of pictures
Old coloring books
Old greeting cards
Wallpaper samples
Wrapping paper—plain and patterned
Aluminum foil
Fabric—all types

### Dioramas and Other Constructions
Boxes—all sizes and shapes
Fabric—all types
Pipe cleaners
Spools
Acorns and other nuts (shells)
Cotton batting
Nets
Moss
Gravel, pebbles, and sand
Sticks
Dried flowers
String, thread, cord, rope, twine, wire
Dried coffee grounds
Toothpicks
Steel wool
Aluminum foil
Tin cans and lids
Brushes
Pine cones
Old jewelry
Wood scraps
Sea shells
Springs
Sponges
Cork
Broom straws
Rickrack
Metal scraps
Tree bark
Egg cartons
Feathers
Milk containers
Fake fur

### Mobile Supports
Wire—various gauges
Dowel rods—all sizes
Wire hangers—cut apart—no hook
Balloon sticks
Cardboard mailing tubes
Twigs and branches
Nylon thread
Nylon fish line
Thin wire

### Mosaics
Cereals—all types and shapes
Dried beans, peas
Seeds—all types
Macaroni—uncooked—all shapes
Colored gravel
Colored rice
Tiles
Broken glass, pottery, dishes (be sure edges are smooth)
Old costume jewelry
Colored paper
Fabric
Buttons
Canceled stamps

### Puppets
Paper plates
Cardboard tubes
Fake fur
Doilies
Buttons
Rickrack
Feathers
Paper—all types
Fabric—all types
Straw
Netting
Yarn
Socks
Sticks
Light bulbs
Paper bags

Some projects require materials that need to be purchased. These supplies should be purchased as needed. Parents are very often willing to buy needed supplies if the project is explained to them and they are given sufficient time to make the purchases.

There are materials you should have on hand, and others need to be purchased. Scissors, glue (Elmer's is best), tape, construction paper (9" x 12" and 12" x 18")—all colors, drawing paper, paint (acrylics are best), brushes, colored tissue and cellophane, clear shellac.

# Appendix II: Basic Recipes

**Sawdust Modeling Mixture**
½ cup sawdust
½ cup plaster of paris
¼ cup wheat paste
1 cup water

Stir mixture thoroughly to blend all ingredients.

**Bread Dough (BAKER'S CLAY)**
1. Mix 4 cups unsifted flour, 1 cup salt and 1½ cups water. Knead for 5 minutes.

Bake finished pieces in a 350 degree oven for 1 hour or until done. (These are NOT edible!)

Clay can be kept in plastic bags. If it dries out, add a bit of water. Clay can be used as modeling clay or rolled out with a rolling pin and cut with knife or cookie cutters.

2. Mix 3 slices of white bread (no crust) with 3 tablespoons of white glue. Knead until bread no longer sticks to fingers.

Allow finished pieces to air dry. Coat with a solution of equal parts of white glue and water.

**Laminating Solution**
Mix ½ container of heavy white craft glue with the same amount of water. Brush on with a soft brush. Several coats will give a hard finish.

**Papier Mâché Mash**
Cover newspaper scraps with water and soak overnight. Knead the soaked mass and squeeze out the excess water through a strainer. Add glue and mix thoroughly. Mixture should not be too sloppy.